Dec. 1, 2004

IMMACULATE CONCEPTION
and the
HOLY SPIRIT

Marian Teachings
of St. Maximilian Kolbe

IMMACULATE CONCEPTION
and the
HOLY SPIRIT

Marian Teachings
of St. Maximilian Kolbe

Fr. H.M. Manteau-Bonamy, OP

Translated from the French by
Bro. Richard Arnandez, FSC

Revised Edition

Marytown Press
1600 West Park Avenue
Libertyville, Illinois 60048
847-367-7800

Original French title: *La Doctrine Mariale du Père Kolbe: Esprit-Saint et Conception Immaculée*
Original publisher: Editions P. Lethielleux, Paris
©1975, Editions Dessain et Tolra, Paris

Imprimatur: E. Berrar, ep. vicar.
　　　　　　　Paris, January 9, 1975

English translation published with ecclesiastical approval.

©1977, 2001, Marytown Press
All rights reserved.
First Edition, 1977
Second printing, 1983
Third printing, 1991
Fourth printing, 1993
Second Edition, 2001

ISBN: 0-913382-00-0
LCCCN: 77-93104

Marytown Press
1600 West Park Avenue, Libertyville, Illinois 60048

TABLE OF CONTENTS

FOREWORD
TO THE FIRST EDITION

I AM INDEED HAPPY TO GREET THE APPEARANCE OF FATHER Manteau-Bonamy's book. Having been from an early age closely associated with Father Kolbe, and being responsible today for continuing his work, the Militia of the Immaculata, I had always hoped to see such a book in print.

It answers the question put by so many who, on learning of the life of this Conventual Franciscan, wonder how such a modern saint could have consecrated every instant of his existence to Mary Immaculate, and why he desired that all men, for the sake of their own sanctification and that of others, should consecrate themselves completely to the Most Blessed Virgin under the title of her Immaculate Conception. Father Kolbe was not only an ardent apostle of Christ but also a theologian who sought to find a solid doctrinal basis for his pastoral efforts. With this end in view he strove, without ever slackening his effort, to understand more deeply the dogma of the Immaculate Conception, personified, one may say at Lourdes, where our Lady declared: "I am the Immaculate Conception."

He realized that the mystery of Mary Immaculate had a profound effect not only on the person of Mary herself, but also on her mission within the history of salvation.

For this reason he declared that "face to face with this mystery it is not enough to sing *Tota Pulchra Es, O Maria*. We have to learn to live according to it." As Pope Paul VI says, "he made of devotion to the Mother of Christ, the Woman clothed with the sun, the center of his spirituality, of his apostolate, and of his theology."

I myself tried to study the thought of Blessed Maximilian, and to condense it in a brief doctrinal synthesis, which was published for the first time in 1953. It was not an easy task. As one of his biographers, Albert Wojtczak, says: "This extraordinary man had the faith of a child, reasoned like a philosopher, and saw things like a mystic in ecstasy." How can one feel sure he has grasped a doctrine like this, expressed in terms far from scholastic, even though brilliant and perfectly orthodox?

At first glance some of Father Kolbe's writings produce a certain amazement. More than one reader might think that Blessed Maximilian gives to Mary Immaculate the place that belongs to Christ in the economy of salvation. Still, in our day, after the writings of Pius XII—the Apostolic Constitution *Munificentissimus* (November 1, 1950, where he defined the dogma of the Assumption); the Encyclicals *Fulgens Corona* (1953) and *Ad Coeli Reginam* (1954)—and after the teaching of Vatican II and the Apostolic Exhortations of Paul VI: *Signum Magnum* (1967) and *Marialis Cultus* (1974); finally after the international Mariological Congresses held between 1951 and 1971, such an impression can hardly be justified.

Prior to all this development of Marian doctrine, the tendency was to consider the Immaculate Conception as a mere privilege granted to the Most Blessed Virgin, a sort of spiritual ornament connected with her divine maternity.

In 1954 the Mariologist, J. Lazure declared: "The Immaculate Conception implies in Mary the existence of inexaustible riches which we have not even guessed at up to now. One of the most precious fruits of this Marian year will certainly be to set in motion—100 years after the defiinition of the dogma, 100 years of intense reflections on it—new and progressive discoveries of what this abyss of light and grandeur really means."

We have not done with discovering the effective dynamism of the primary grace given to Mary, a primary grace something like the fertilizing sperm cell at the origin of a new human being. Pius XII believed that all the future glory Mary would enjoy was already implied in her Immaculate Conception. Twenty years earlier, Blessed Maximilian had seemingly foretold that "men would arise who would study and understand much better the Immaculate Conception" (Conversation with Fr. Leon Veuthey in 1933).

Vatican II elucidated the role Mary plays in the Church, a privileged role, even though it remains in total subordination to that of Jesus: "her motherhood in the economy of grace will continue uninterruptedly till all the elect are definitely crowned . . . The Church experiences her help unceasingly, she recommends to the hearts of the faithful that they turn to Mary's patronage, so that her motherly help and protection may lead them all to be ever more closely united to the Mediator and Savior, Christ" (*Lumen Gentium*, n. 62). Again the Council declares: "In Mary the Church admires and extols the most excellent fruit of the Redemption; and in her as in a most pure mirror, the Church contemplates with joy what she herself desires and hopes to be" (*Const. on the Liturgy*, n. 103). To lay people the Council does not hesitate to say: "All should profess towards her (Mary) a true devotion, and should entrust to her maternal solicitude their lives and their apostolic efforts" (*Apost. of Laity*, n. 4).

After hearing such official statements from the Church herself, who can be surprised to find Father Kolbe, a modern apostle who let himself be led by Mary the Queen of Apostles at all times, wanting to "Marianize" and "Immaculatize" the entire world?

Blessed Maximilian's Marian doctrine appears much easier to grasp today, after the Council and the post-conciliar research carried out concerning the union of the Church and of the Most Blessed Virgin, the mother of the Church, with the Holy Spirit. "The Holy Spirit, being one and the same in the Head and in the members, vivifies the whole body, unifies it, moves it, so that his action has been compared by the Fathers to the function fulfilled in a human body by the principle of life, the soul" (*Lumen Gentium*, n. 7).

Pope Paul VI in his recent Apostolic Exhortation *Marialis Cultus* insistently begged the "entire people of God, especially the pastors and the theologians, to deepen their reflections on the action of the Holy Spirit in the history of salvation, and to strive so that the formulas employed by Christian piety should duly illustrate his life-giving influence. Such a deepened understanding should provide a better grasp of the mysterious relationship between the Spirit of God and the Virgin of Nazareth, and their common action in the Church. From these deeper meditations on these truths of faith there arise a piety that will be lived more intensely."

This is exactly what Father Kolbe never tired of saying in his day; he insisted that the era of the Holy Spirit which he thought was drawing near would also be the era of Mary Immaculate. Because of this, far from trying to substitute the Virgin for Christ, Blessed Maximilian joined the mediation of Mary to the mediation of love proper to the second Paraclete. The Council has given to Mary names which express the role of the third Person in the Church: "advocate," "helper," "mediatrix" (cf. *Lumen Gentium*, n. 62).

In line with all this we can see how these considerations enlighten our faith in the universal mediation of Mary Immaculate. One can then understand the answer that Father Kolbe gave to his most original question: "Who then are you, O Immaculate Conception?"

In his testament-document written on February 17, 1941, he declares that Mary took the very name of the Holy Spirit, who is the uncreated Immaculate Conception, because she is his spouse, his handmaid, his sanctuary. Thus, inseparable from the Holy Spirit as from her Son, Mary Immaculate is always present wherever the Spirit is.

This is what Father Manteau-Bonamy brings out so well here. He was an expert at the Council, and has written a book on the same theme: *The Virgin Mary and the Holy Spirit.* Professor Jean Guitton says of him that he is one of those who, in our day, "have penetrated the depths of meaning contained in these words, forever rich and mysterious: '*to pneuma, to aghion*!' (the Spirit, the Holy One)."

What does Father Manteau-Bonamy tell us that will bring us nearer to the solution of the problem that Father Kolbe outlined some twenty-five years prior to the Council?

First, he observes that Father Kolbe is a theologian whose teaching is perfectly sound, a pioneer in the field of Mariological study. Next, he deserves credit for explicitating the theological intuitions found in Father Kolbe's writings.

Finally, he draws attention to the fact that Father Kolbe, by showing the unity of action between the Holy Spirit and the Most Blessed Virgin, succeeded in making much clearer the how and the why of Mary's universal mediation, and in so doing has, we hope, removed the last remaining obstacle holding up the definition of this truth as a dogma, something he desired with all his heart.

I hope that this work will meet with the widest possible success; that it will be read by theologians whom it should stimulate to continue working along the lines inspired by Blessed Maximilian; and also all Christians who, by meditating on the thoughts of Father Kolbe, will see their own spiritual life deepened, and their apostolate made ever more fruitful.

FR. GEORGE DOMANSKI, OFM CONV.
INTERNATIONAL DIRECTOR, MILITIA OF THE IMMACULATA
ROME, DECEMBER 8, 1974

FOREWORD
TO THE SECOND EDITION

The only knowledge that is of value is that which proceeds from love. . . . Our knowledge of the Immaculata must bring forth fruit in sacrifice; the greater the sacrifice, the greater love it proves.   St. Maximilian Kolbe

ONE WILL NEVER UNDERSTAND THE LENGTH AND DEPTH, the height and breadth, of the relationship and union between the Holy Spirit and the Immaculate Virgin Mary through study alone. To even begin to understand St. Maxmilian Kolbe's insights and writings on the Holy Spirit and the Immaculate Conception one must have experienced Love: the love between a parent and child, or husband and wife, or best of friends, but most of all the love of God that transcends all other loves, for the relationship between the Holy Spirit and the Immaculate Virgin Mary transcends the intellect and reason.

God's choosing of the Virgin Mary to be the Mother of God (*Théotokos*), was not an intellectual choice alone but primarily an act of love, for God is Love and thus all of God's actions are acts of love. When the Word became flesh, the Holy Spirit over-shadowed the Immaculate Virgin Mary and the two (the Holy Spirit and Mary) became not one flesh but one in spirit, united in mind, heart and soul. She to whom we consecrate ourselves is the ultimate consecration herself.

In her we find the one person who perfectly fulfilled her consecration to God. Never did she desire nor will anything contrary to the will of God. She was the perfect instrument, possession and property of God. Never has the human heart given itself so freely, so totally and so absolutely to God. Her union with the Holy Spirit is total and complete. It is a union of the mind, heart, soul and body with the Holy Spirit. This union can never be fully explained in words or expressed in intellectual terms. Only those who have fallen in love with God and have no envy in their hearts can begin to grasp the love between the Holy Spirit and the Immaculate Virgin. It is a love where one seeks only what the other seeks; a love that wills only what the other wills; a love that unites one to the other totally and absolutely without any separation whatso-ever; a love so total and unitive and intimate it is "almost" as if there is no distinction between them.

This is why the Holy Spirit and the Immaculate Virgin can act as one, always in total harmony and union. They never act separately or apart from the other because their union is total, absolute, irrevocable and eternal.

But their love is not exclusive. It is the first great love be-tween God and his creatures after which all other loves be-tween God and man are modeled. It is a love that is open to all who consecrate themselves to God through the Immaculate Virgin, for through consecration one enters into, and partici-pates in, the same intimate union of love between the Holy Spirit and Mary. It is a love that will be experienced by all in the Kingdom of Heaven at the heavenly wedding banquet where the Bride, the Church, will be forever wedded to her groom, Christ the Lord. Then and only then will we understand the unity and the love between the Holy Spirit and the Immaculate Virgin Mary and thus the unity and love of all mankind with God in the Kingdom that it foreshadows.

Therefore read this book with Love!

FR. PATRICK GREENOUGH, OFM CONV.
NATIONAL PRESIDENT, MILITIA OF THE IMMACULATA
FEAST OF OUR LADY OF THE ROSARY
OCTOBER 7, 2000

Introduction

I T MUST BE REPEATED OVER AND OVER AGAIN THAT THE ENTIRE life of Father Kolbe was spent in the pursuit of a single goal: making Mary Immaculate known and loved, so that all men might realize to the full what their Christian vocation implies.

To achieve this he never hesitated to use all possible means: preaching, the printed word, radio. He wore himself out in this task, and in the end he gave his life itself.

Especially during his sojourn in Japan did Father Kolbe often mention his desire to write a book on Mary Immaculate.

Sometimes, the notion comes to me to write something more extensive about the Most Blessed Virgin, a little book concerned with dogma, profound yet simple at the same time. (Letter to Fr. Cornelius Czupryk)

Again:

If Mary Immaculate so wills, we shall found a Marian Academy, to study, teach and publicize everywhere who Mary Immaculate really is. (Letter to Fr. Antonio Vivoda)

In fact, as many witnesses can testify, he often exclaimed sorrowfully: "How little known Mary Immaculate still is!" This idea of a deeper study of the question became more and more of an obsession with him, despite his lack of time and his poor health. In a letter addressed to his Brothers at the Polish "City of the Immaculata" Father Kolbe gave some details of what he had in mind, and developed his plan to some extent.

> We must neglect nothing so that the Immaculata may be ever better known. Her relationships with the Father, the Son and the Holy Spirit, with the Trinity as a whole, with Jesus, with the Angels and with us must be made clear . . . . We have here an unlimited field for study.
>
> Then we must find ways of presenting the result of these studies to each and to all, through preaching, the press, radio. . . .
>
> We know so little as yet about all that the Immaculata has done for the human race, from the first instant of her existence to this very day. . . . Every grace given to us has passed through her hands. . . .
>
> And all this must be proposed to souls so that they may be nourished with the Immaculata . . . so that they might resemble her as soon as possible, and be changed into her. Then they will love Jesus with the Immaculata's heart." (Letter to Niepokalanow, October 30, 1935)

This is the approach that Father Manteau-Bonamy has adopted in his work, in order to fulfill Father Kolbe's wish and to give to every well-disposed reader a "more fully worked-out doctrinal presentation of his thought" (cf. *Entretiens spirituels inédits du Bienheureux Pére M. Kolbe, P. Lethielleux*, 1974 p. 20).

A year before his death Father Kolbe set down on paper some ideas on this topic and sketched plans for this book. For the most part these texts bear dates between August 5 and August 20, 1940. Other fragments of the same kind are scattered throughout his writings dating back to 1938, 1939, the beginning of 1940 and on into 1941. We can consider all these extracts as a sort of preliminary "sketch" of the main chapters that would have made up Father Kolbe's "Marian Summa."[1] Thus, Father Kolbe was laboriously gathering his material, like a careful and conscientious worker; like the wise man in the Gospel he knew how to draw out of his treasure house "new things and old."

But death stalked the "Knight of the Immaculata." On February 17, 1941, Father Maximilian was arrested by the Nazis. That very day he had written one of his most moving pages on the Immaculata and the three divine Persons. This text—the last piece of writing from his pen that we possess—is the only one that contains the statement: "The Holy Spirit is the uncreated Immaculate Conception." It is, without doubt, the clear and definitive answer to the question which Father Kolbe had been asking himself for so long: "Who then are you, O Immaculate Conception?" As can be seen from the documents at the end of this book, during 1938, 1939 and 1940 he was still trying to clear up in his own mind the meaning of "conception," and how this term could be understood in God himself. The text which he wrote on February 17, 1941 is quoted in part in the *Entretiens spirituels* cited above, and in full in the first chapter of the present work.

After his death, his work once again developed according to the designs of Providence. All the texts cited and studied here by Father Manteau-Bonamy had been gathered and published, in particular in the critical Polish edition of his writings. For years most of them had remained more or less ignored. Now they are being brought to light little by little; and they show the wealth of Father Kolbe's contemplation.

---

[1] The quotations from these texts used in this book will be entitled "Sketch," with the appropriate date. The greater part of these excerpts will be published integrally in the Appendices to this volume.

Two days before his arrest, on February 15, 1941, Father Kolbe was talking to some of his fellow religious, and once again he revealed to them, very discreetly, the depths of his soul.

Science puffs up; it can be useful in so far as it serves charity. Satan knows a lot more theology than any of us, but it does him no good. The only knowledge that is of value is that which proceeds from love. . . . In fact, our knowledge of the Immaculata must bring forth fruit in sacrifice; the greater the sacrifice, the greater love it proves.

What a splendid commentary on St. Paul's words: "Science indeed puffs up, but charity edifies." Thanks to these unguarded words we can surmise the supernatural climate of detachment and love in which Father Kolbe was working at his book on the Immaculata. His is the typical way of acting we find in the saints, the mystics who "have crucified their flesh" to let themselves be "led by the Spirit" of truth and love (Gal 5:10, 24).

Father Kolbe was distrustful not so much of human reason as of human pride, which seldom fails to infiltrate intellectual pursuits. In a letter to Brother Mikolajczyk he gives a remarkable example of the attitude which was his; although he was about to put forward with boldness the ineffable link between the Holy Spirit and Mary Immaculate, he indicates his manner of proceeding, which is so wise in all circumstances.

It is a fine thing to study Mariology; but let us never forget that we will get to understand Mary much better through humble prayer, through the loving experience of our daily lives, than through learned definitions, distinctions and arguments, even though we must not neglect these latter.

Thus did he pitch his efforts on the right plane.

Through his careful and fervent efforts, Father Manteau-Bonamy has traced out for us the path followed by Father

Kolbe in his mariological study. These writings, from 1938 to 1941, make up a section apart in the totality of Father Kolbe's works. If we have the good fortune to possess them all, it is due to the fact that Father Maximilian wished to lay down clearly the Marian convictions that underlay his own spiritual and apostolic life.

The Brothers of Niepokalanow in Poland always took great care to preserve everything Father Kolbe wrote. This is why it has been possible to collect the various items which have been printed under the title *Entretiens spirituels inédits*, published by Lethielleux.

What do they contain?

Father Kolbe was always a man who kept in touch with others, who liked to share with his Brothers the things which he had most at heart.

We possess a considerable number of his letters addressed to his family—his mother and his brother—and to his religious Brothers in Poland, Japan and Italy. Father Kolbe never wrote much of set purpose, he wrote as the occasion offered, answering as definitely as he could the questions that arose. Hence all his correspondence displays a lively, unrehearsed style; all sorts of things are touched upon: material concerns and spiritual preoccupations. Thus, while we hear echoes of his active existence in the midst of whirring presses, we also get glimpses of his soul's life, ever seeking to draw closer and closer to Mary Immaculate, and through her to the Blessed Trinity.

Whenever he could, Father Kolbe also liked to converse face to face with people, especially his Brothers. From 1927 onward he was in the habit of giving them talks at Niepokalanow. Then, after definitively leaving Japan in 1936, and until his arrest, he undertook the task of giving spiritual conferences to his community of some 750 members. Almost daily he spoke on some religious topic, and likewise gave practical directions for the proper functioning of the institution. On reading these talks, so simple yet so sublime at times, one can scarcely help thinking of St. Vincent de Paul speaking to his priests and to the Sisters of Charity.

The saints have the secret of speaking to us of things which are ineffable. They are ever attentive to the voice of the Holy Spirit, "who intercedes for us with unspeakable groanings" (Rom 8:26).

Guided by his love of Mary Immaculate, Father Kolbe seldom failed to discuss, in his letters or in his talks, one or the other of the great Mariological themes: the Immaculata and her relationships with the Blessed Trinity, her motherhood; her mediation; her royalty of love over all souls, etc. We have a fairly complete echo of all this in the *Entretiens spirituels inédits.* Father Manteau-Bonamy's theological reflections are based on these texts.

A man's thought makes up a unified whole; but often enough it takes years for this whole to shape up in his mind. Father Kolbe is above all a contemplative who is at the same time a realist, who looks at spiritual truths squarely in order to live by them himself and to find in them the spiritual nourishment needed by his Brothers. This is why the letters and conferences from the years before 1940 are so important. The major documents written in August 1940 are, so to speak, the conclusions drawn from years of searching in prayer and sacrifice.

Father Kolbe forged steadily ahead in his discovery of Mary's mystery. The book he wanted to write would have had to be the result of spiritual experience, firmly based on dogmatic truth. No place here for pious sentimentality; only one thing mattered really: the truth discovered in love.

REV. J. F. VILLEPELÉE

DESIGNATIONS USED IN THE REFERENCES

Conferences: Talks given by Father Maximilian and summarized by Brothers who heard them.

Knight of the Immaculata: The monthly magazine published at Niepokalanow.

Miles Immaculatae: A quarterly periodical for priests published in Latin.

Sketch: Material written by Father Maximilian which he was collecting for a book.

Notes: Ideas, etc., which St. Maximilian either wrote down in his own hand or dictated in a precise way.

St. Maximilian Kolbe:
Biography & Chronology

St. Maximilian Kolbe
"Prophet of the Civilization of Love"

S T. MAXIMILIAN KOLBE, OFM CONV., WAS BORN IN POLAND IN 1894. As a seminarian in Rome he witnessed a well-organized demonstration by Freemasons against the Catholic Church beneath the very windows of the Vatican. This event inspired him to found the Militia of the Immaculata (MI) evangelization movement in October 1917.

Kolbe's method of outreach was to encourage each and every individual to make a total consecration to Mary. This act of abandonment would result in personal sanctification, the conversion of Church opponents and ultimately the establishment of the universal reign of the Sacred Heart of Jesus Christ.

After being ordained a priest, Father Maximilian began forming MI prayer groups and publishing a magazine, *Knight of the Immaculata*. The publishing ministry grew so rapidly that in 1927 he built an evangelization center near Warsaw called

Niepokalanow (City of the Immaculata). By the time of the Nazi invasion of Poland in 1939, the City was home to 650 friars and was the largest Catholic religious house in the world.

Kolbe utilized the most modern printing and administrative techniques available, enabling he and his friars to publish a daily newspaper and a number of periodicals. *The Knight* reached a circulation of nearly one million. Niepokalanow became the largest Catholic publishing house in Poland and perhaps in the world.

In his zeal to "win the world for the Immaculata," Kolbe, in 1930, established a missionary center in Japan and had plans for centers in India and China. He built an airstrip to better distribute his newspapers, used short wave radio, and drew up plans for evangelizing through television and films.

While the Gestapo was thundering toward Niepokalanow to whisk him away to the death camp, Father Kolbe hurried to complete his essay on Mary's self-title at Lourdes, France, "I am the Immaculate Conception." His keen insights further developed the Church's centuries-old teaching that the Blessed Virgin, Spouse of the Holy Spirit, is the Mediatrix, or "gateway" of all the graces that flow to mankind from the Trinity. Pope Paul VI called St. Maximilian "clairvoyant" in his anticipation of the Marian theology of the Second Vatican Council, and Pope John Paul II has proclaimed him "apostle of a new Marian era."

In 1992, the Holy Father evolved our understanding of Kolbe's spirituality even further. By dying for another and "consecrating his life to the Immaculate Virgin," St. Maximilian has become for us "a sign and a prophet of the new era, the civilization of love." Here Pope John Paul II is clearly endorsing the Kolbean example of Marian consecration as a critical element of his "new evangelization" for the third Christian millennium, and St. Maximilian as a primary intercessor.

Father Maximilian was imprisoned in the Nazi concentra-

St. Maximilian Maria Kolbe
January 8, 1894—August 14, 1941

tion camp of Auschwitz in 1941, where he was singled out for special brutalities as a Catholic priest. In a supreme act of love, he defended the right to life of a prisoner who had been condemned to a starvation bunker by offering to take his place. Two weeks later, on August 14, 1941, Kolbe's impatient captors ended his life by a fatal injection. Pope John Paul II canonized him a saint and "martyr of charity" in 1982.

St. Maximilian Kolbe is the patron of families, journalists, prisoners, the pro-life movement and, because of his manner of death, the chemically addicted and those with eating disorders. He is truly the saint of our difficult modern era, and a splendid model for all people of good will throughout the next Christian millennium.

A Chronology

January 8, 1894: Raymond Kolbe is born at Zdunska Wola, Poland, of Julius and Maria Dabrowska. He is baptized the same day, at the parish church of the Assumption of the Blessed Virgin Mary.

June 29, 1902: He receives his First Communion of the parish church of St. Matthew in Pabianice, where the family had moved, looking for better work as weavers.

1907: Attracted by the preaching of a Conventual Franciscan priest at a parish mission in Pabianice, Raymond and his brother, Francis, enter the high school seminary of the Conventual Franciscans in Lwow.

1908: Maria Kolbe, with the consent of her husband, leaves the world and begins living with the Benedictine Sisters of Lwow, and from 1913, with the Felician Sisters of Krakow, as a tertiary and oblate.

September 4, 1910: Raymond enters the Conventual Franciscan novitiate at Lwow, and is given the name Friar Maximilian.

November 10, 1912: He is sent to the Order's seminary in Rome, the International Seraphic College, and begins his philosophical studes at the Gregorian University.

Sept-Oct 1914: Julius Kolbe, an officer in the Polish Army, is taken prisoner with his squad by the Russian occupation forces and is executed.

November 1, 1914: Friar Maximilian makes his solemn profession as a Franciscan religious in the seminary chapel.

October 22, 1915: He receives his doctorate in philosophy from the Gregorian.

January 20 1917: It is the seventy-fifth anniversary of the apparition of the Immaculata to the Jewish agnostic, Alphonse

Ratisbonne. Inspired by the conversion story during morning meditation in the seminary chapel, Friar Maximilian resolves to found a Marian association.

October 16, 1917: With six fellow friars at the Order's seminary, he founds the Militia of the Immaculata (MI).

April 28, 1918: Friar Maximilian is ordained a priest, at the church of Sant'Andrea della Valle, Rome.

April 29, 1918: Father Maximilian celebrates his first Mass in the church of Sant'Andrea delle Fratte, Rome, at the altar where the Immaculata appeared to Alphonse Ratisbonne in 1842.

March 28, 1919: Pope Benedict XV blesses the MI by word of mouth at the request of Archbishop Dominic Jaquet.

April 4, 1919: Vicar General of the Order, Fr. Dominic Tavani, blesses and confirms the MI in writing.

July 22, 1919: Fr. Maximilian receives his doctorate in theology at the Pontifical Theological Faculty of St. Bonaventure in Rome.

July 29, 1919: He is assigned to the Order's seminary in Krakow, and begins teaching Church history in October.

August 11, 1920: He journeys to Zakopane, Poland, to receive treatment for tuberculosis of the lungs. He functions as a chaplain at the hospital, and is discharged April 28, 1921.

January 2, 1922: The MI is approved as a Pious Union by the Vicar General of the Archdiocese of Rome, Cardinal Basil Pompilii.

January 1922: Maximilian prints at Krakow the first issue of the MI's magazine, *Rycerz Niepokalanej* (*Knight of the Immaculata*), with a press run of 5,000.

October 20, 1922: The offices of the *Knight* are transferred to the seminary at Grodno, Poland.

December 1922: The January 1923 edition is printed, using an obsolete manual press, with a press run of 12,000.

September 18, 1926: Father Maximilian returns to Zakopane for more treatment for tuberculosis, which ends in April 1927.

November 20, 1926: Pope Pius XI blesses the *Knight* on the fifth anniversary of its founding.

December 18, 1926: Pope Pius XI grants indulgences to the MI, which is canonically erected at the International Seraphic College, Rome.

July 1927: Father Maximilian begins negotiations with Prince Drucki-Lubecki to obtain a tract of land at Teresin, near Warsaw, to build a new friary and publishing center.

August 6, 1927: Blessing of a statue of the Immaculata on the terrain of the future friary.

October 1927: Construction of the center begins, with canonical erection of the friary, called Niepokalanow. The Franciscan religious family consists of two priests and eighteen friars, with Father Maximilian as guardian (superior). In the next twelve years, it would grow to about seven hundred members who would operate the largest publishing establishment in Central Europe.

Jan 14-Feb 5, 1930: Father Maximilian pilgrimages to shrines throughout Europe, including Lourdes, to spiritually prepare for the establishment of a foreign mission in the Far East.

February 26, 1930: With three fellow friars, he leaves for Nagasaki, Japan.

May 24, 1930: One month after their arrival, the first issue of the Japanese *Knight of the Immaculata*, *Seibo no Kishi*, is published with a press run of 10,000. Father Maximilian also teaches philosophy at the Nagasaki seminary.

May 16, 1931: The editorial offices of the *Kishi* are transferred from a rented house to purchased land at the base of Nagasaki's Mt. Hikosan. They name the new friary is *Mugenzai no Sono*, the Garden of the Immaculata.

May 29-July 24, 1932: Father Maximilian travels to India to investigate the possibility of founding a third Niepokalanow.

July 13, 1936: He returns to Poland to participate in the provincial chapter, and is named guardian of Niepokalanow.

December 8, 1937: The first shortwave radio transmissions from Niepokalanow are initiated, with the call number SP 3 RN (Polish Station 3 Radio Niepokalanow). Books and periodicals are being published in several languages. Catholic films are in the planning.

September 1, 1939: The Nazis invade Poland, and WWII breaks out. Father Maximilian and thirty-seven brothers are arrested and interned at three prison camps.

December 8, 1939: He and his confreres are set free on the feast of the Immaculate Conception.

November 20, 1940: Surprisingly, the Nazis give Maximilian permission to print one, final issue of the *Knight*, with a press run of 120,000.

February 17, 1941: Father Maximilian and four friars are arrested by the Gestapo and sent to Pawiak prison in Warsaw.

May 28, 1941: He arrives with a trainload of prisoners at Auschwitz, and is assigned the registration number 16,670.

July 28-Aug 1, 1941: During this five-day period, Fritsch, the commandant, sentences ten prisoners from Block 14 to death by starvation in retaliation for the escape of a prisoner from the block. Father Maximilian offers to take the place of one of the condemned, Sgt. Francis Gajonwniczek, which is accepted. The ten prisoners are placed in the underground starvation bunker in Block 13.

August 14, 1941: Still alive after two weeks, Father Maximilian and three survivors are killed by an injection of carbolic acid. His body is burned in the crematorium the next day, the feast of the Assumption.

March 17, 1946: Maria Kolbe passes away at Krakow, at age seventy-six.

August 12, 1947: The Apostolic See authorizes the beginning of the informative process for the beatification of Servant of God, Father Maximilian Kolbe.

January 30, 1969: Pope Paul VI declares the Servant of God a "victim of charity," and proclaims him Venerable.

October 17, 1971: Pope Paul VI, in Rome, proclaims Venerable Maximilian Kolbe "Blessed."

October 10, 1982: Pope John Paul II, in Rome, proclaims Blessed Maximilian a Saint of the Church, calling him a "martyr of charity."

October 16, 1997: On the seventieth anniversary of the founding of the Militia of the Immaculata, the Holy See, through the Pontifical Council for the Laity, approves the revised International Governing Statutes of the MI. It then erects the MI as an international public association of the faithful. This is the most esteemed recognition the Church can bestow upon a lay organization.

Chapter 1

"I AM THE IMMACULATE CONCEPTION"

A few hours before his second and final arrest, on February 17, 1941, Father Kolbe had time to put on paper his thoughts about her who for a quarter of a century, day after day, had never ceased to occupy his priestly and apostolic mind and heart. This text is, therefore, of the highest importance. Evidently, he could not have written it during his captivity at Pawiak near Warsaw, nor during his detention in the death camp at Auschwitz.[1] In these lines we find the gist of his Marian doctrine—a doctrine that he would have wished to work out in more ample form. We possess several sketches of this projected book, dating back mostly to the years 1939-41.

This last writing of Father Kolbe constitutes his spiritual testament. Let us try to follow the line of his reasoning; in so doing we shall be sure to remain faithful to his thought.

IMMACULATE CONCEPTION. These words fell from the lips of the Immaculata herself. Hence, they must tell us in the most precise and essential manner who she really is.

Since human words are incapable of expressing divine realities, it follows that these words: "Immaculate," and "Conception" must be understood in a much more profound, much more beautiful and sublime meaning than usual:

a meaning beyond that which human reason at its most penetrating, commonly gives to them.

St. Paul wrote, quoting the Prophet Isaiah: "'Things that the eye has not seen, that the ear has not heard, that the heart of man has not imagined' (Is 64:4), such are the good things that God has prepared for those who love him" (1 Cor 2:9). Here, these words apply fully.

However, we can and should reverently inquire into the mystery of the Immaculata and try to express it with words provided by our intelligence using its own proper powers.

Who then are you, O Immaculate Conception?

Not God, of course, because he has no beginning. Not an angel, created directly out of nothing. Not Adam, formed out of the dust of the earth (Gen 2:7). Not Eve, moulded from Adam's rib (Gen 2:21). Not the Incarnate Word, who exists before all ages, and of whom we should use the word "conceived" rather than "conception." Humans do not exist before their conception, so we might call them created "conceptions." But you, O Mary, are different from all other children of Eve. They are conceptions stained by original sin; whereas you are the unique, Immaculate Conception.

Everything which exists, outside of God himself, since it is from God and depends on him in every way, bears within itself some semblance to its Creator; there is nothing in any creature which does not betray this resemblance, because every created thing is an effect of the Primal Cause.

It is true that the words we use to speak of created realities express the divine perfections only in a halting, limited and analogical manner. They are only a more or less distant echo—as are the created realities that they signify—of the properties of God himself.

Would not "conception" be an exception to this rule? No; there is never any such exception.

The Father begets the Son; the Spirit proceeds from Father and Son. These few words sum up the mystery of the life of the Most Blessed Trinity and of all the perfections in creatures which are nothing else but echoes, a hymn of praise, a many-hued tableau, of this primary and most wondrous of all mysteries.

We must perforce use our customary vocabulary, since it is all we have; but we must never forget that our vocabulary is very inadequate.

Who is the Father? What is his personal life like? It consists in begetting, eternally; because he begets his Son from the beginning, and forever.

Who is the Son? He is the Begotten-One, because from the beginning and for all eternity he is begotten by the Father.

And who is the Holy Spirit? The flowering of the love of the Father and the Son. If the fruit of created love is a created conception, then the fruit of divine Love, that prototype of all created love, is necessarily a divine "conception." The Holy Spirit is, therefore, the "uncreated, eternal conception," the prototype of all the conceptions that multiply life throughout the whole universe.

The Father begets; the Son is begotten; the Spirit is the "conception" that springs from their love; there we have the intimate life of the three Persons by which they can be distinguished one from another. But they are united in the oneness of their Nature, of their divine existence.

The Spirit is, then, this thrice holy "conception," this infinitely holy, Immaculate Conception.

Everywhere in this world we notice action, and the reaction which is equal but contrary to it; departure and return; going away and coming back; separation and reunion. The separation always looks forward to union, which is creative. All this is simply an image of the Blessed Trinity

3

in the activity of creatures. Union means love, creative love. Divine activity, outside the Trinity itself, follows the same pattern. First, God creates the universe; that is something like a separation. Creatures, by following the natural law implanted in them by God, reach their perfection, become like him, and go back to him. Intelligent creatures love him in a conscious manner; through this love they unite themselves more and more closely with him, and so find their way back to him. The creature most completely filled with this love, filled with God himself, was the Immaculata, who never contracted the slightest stain of sin, who never departed in the least from God's will. United to the Holy Spirit as his spouse, she is one with God in an incomparably more perfect way than can be predicated of any other creature.

What sort of union is this? It is above all an interior union, a union of her essence with the "essence" of the Holy Spirit. The Holy Spirit dwells in her, lives in her. This was true from the first instant of her existence. It was always true; it will always be true.

In what does this life of the Spirit in Mary consist? He himself is uncreated Love in her; the Love of the Father and of the Son, the Love by which God loves himself, the very love of the Most Holy Trinity. He is a fruitful Love, a "Conception." Among creatures made in God's image the union brought about by married love is the most intimate of all (cf. Mt 19:6). In a much more precise, more interior, more essential manner, the Holy Spirit lives in the soul of the Immaculata, in the depths of her very being. He makes her fruitful, from the very first instant of her existence, all during her life, and for all eternity.

This eternal "Immaculate Conception" (which is the Holy Spirit) produces in an immaculate manner divine life itself in the womb (or depths) of Mary's soul, making her the Immaculate Conception, the human Immaculate Conception. And the virginal womb of Mary's body is kept sacred for him; there he conceives in time—because everything that is material occurs in time—the human life of the Man-God.

And so the return to God (which is love), that is to say the equal and contrary reaction, follows a different path from that found in creation. The path of creation goes from the Father through the Son and by the Holy Spirit; this return trail goes from the Spirit through the Son back to the Father; in other words, by the Spirit the Son becomes incarnate in the womb of the Immaculata; and through this Son love returns to the Father.

And she (the Immaculata), grafted into the Love of the Blessed Trinity, becomes from the first moment of her existence and forever thereafter the "complement of the Blessed Trinity."

In the Holy Spirit's union with Mary we observe more than the love of two beings; in one there is all the love of the Blessed Trinity; in the other, all of creation's love. So it is that in this union heaven and earth are joined; all of heaven with all the earth, the totality of eternal love with the totality of created love. It is truly the summit of love.

At Lourdes, the Immaculata did not say of herself that she had been conceived immaculately, but, as St. Bernadette repeated it, "*Que soy era immaculada councepciou*": "I am the Immaculate Conception."

If among human beings the wife takes the name of her husband because she belongs to him, is one with him, becomes equal to him and is, with him, the source of new life, with how much greater reason should the name of the Holy Spirit, who is the divine Immaculate Conception, be used as the name of her in whom he lives as uncreated Love, the principle of life in the whole supernatural order of grace? (Sketch, February 17, 1941)

Father Kolbe's whole reason for living, suffering and dying was to meditate on the answer given by our Lady to St. Bernadette when she was asked to identify herself, so that he might live by it himself, and get others to do the same.

It would be tedious to count the number of times Father Kolbe repeated without tiring:

> When our Blessed Mother was asked by Bernadette to tell her name, she answered: "I am the Immaculate Conception"; this is the Immaculata's definition of herself. (Conference, July 26, 1931)

For this reason, in his Beatification homily Pope Paul VI did not hesitate to declare:

> Maximilian Kolbe was an apostle of the formal veneration of Mary seen in her primary, original and privileged splendor: that of the definition she gave of herself at Lourdes. (October 17, 1971)

In this expression of our Lady, Father Kolbe found a revelation of the mystery so deeply hidden in Mary. He would have wished to found a Marian Academy where theologians would study Mary not only for the sake of simple, abstract truth, but also with a view to bringing souls back to God.

> Who and what is the Immaculata? Who can understand her perfectly? Mary is the Mother of God, the Immaculate One, or better yet, the Immaculate Conception as she wished to be known at Lourdes. We all understand what "mother" means; but "Mother of God" is something that our reason and our limited intellect cannot really grasp. So too, only God really understands what "immaculate" means. "Conceived without sin" we can fathom up to a point; but "Immaculate Conception" is an expression that abounds in the most consoling mysteries.
>
> If the Immaculata so wills it, we shall found an Academy

of Mariology in order to study, teach and publish throughout the world what the mystery of the Immaculata really contains. We shall have an Academy delivering diplomas in Mariology. This is as yet a largely unexplored field; yet it is very necessary to work at it for the sake of its importance in everyday life, in the task of converting and sanctifying souls." (Letter to Fr. Anthony Vivoda, April 4, 1933)

With the name *Immaculate Conception*, Mary gave us the secret of her heart.

This name must be very dear to her, because it indicates the special grace that lies at the source of her being, the grace which she received at the first instant of her existence. As we know, the first gift is always the one we cherish most. (Sketch, 1940)

In this name she also gave us the secret of her very nature.

In her apparition at Lourdes she does not say: "I was conceived immaculately"; but "I am the Immaculate Conception." This points up not only the fact that she was conceived without sin, but also the manner in which this privilege belongs to her. It is not something accidental; it is something that belongs to her very nature. For she is Immaculate Conception in person.[2] (Letter from Nagasaki to the youth of the Franciscan Order, February 28, 1933)

More than once Father Kolbe compares this statement by our Lady to the affirmation God addressed to Moses on Mt. Horeb: "I am he who is."

When Bernadette repeated her request the Immaculata revealed her true name by saying "I am the Immaculate Conception." To no one but her does such a name apply. When God revealed his name to Moses, he declared: "I am he who is" (Ex 3:14), because God exists from eternity and to eternity. His essence is limitless Being, beyond all time and under all aspects. Whatever exists outside of God himself cannot be said to be being *in se*; it receives its being from him. Thus, the Immaculata also began to exist in time. (Sketch, 1940)

If he compares the "I am" uttered by God and the "I am" pronounced by Mary, it is because he is trying to show the infinite difference between God and the noblest of his creatures.

"Immaculate Conception" does not mean, as some have thought, that the most Blessed Virgin had no earthly father. She came, like all other children of our race, from a human family; she had a true father and a true mother.

We say that she was conceived; hence she is not God, who has no beginning; nor is she an angel created immediately by God. . . . Further, she calls herself "conception," but not after the fashion of Jesus, who even though he was conceived, exists as God from all eternity.

But she is "Immaculate Conception." This is what sets her apart from all other children of Adam. Hence the name Immaculate Conception belongs to her, and to her alone. (Sketch, 1940)

Mary is, then, immaculate in her conception, i.e. conceived without any stain of sin, preserved from Original Sin by the anticipated application of the merits of her Son. Such is the theological formulation of the dogma defined in 1854 by Pope Pius IX, some four years prior to her apparition at Lourdes. In the fact that at Lourdes she called herself "Immaculate Conception," we find a manner of expressing the mystery of her immaculate conception which, at first sight, does not seem to follow from the dogmatic definition. This name that the Virgin attributes to herself, as though defining who she is, seems to go beyond her, to divinize her so to speak. Here we find ourselves in the very heart of the problem that Father Kolbe

8

sought, all through his life, to unravel.

This name cannot be merely symbolic, reflecting in an imaginative way Mary's position in the heart of the Blessed Trinity. But what then is the reality hidden beneath this expression, which taken literally, it would hardly be proper to apply to a mere creature?

Let us turn to the story of the apparitions; we shall see that the question had already arisen on that 25th of March, 1858.

She the (Lady) let her beads hang from her right arm. Her hands which had been joined she first separated then stretched out toward the earth. From this simple gesture a sort of majesty radiated. Her silhouette, like that of a young girl, seemed suffused with grandeur; her countenance shone with the brightness of eternal youth. Then, with a single movement she joined her hands again at the level of her breast, raised her eyes to heaven, and said: *"Que soy era Immaculada Councepciou."*

Immediately after the apparition, [when Bernadette repeated this to the parish priest of Lourdes,] he staggered under the impact of the words, even though he did not yet realize their full scope. His words tumbled out, harsh and to the point:

"A lady can't have such a name as that!

He tried to remember his theology, the articles he had read four years previously at the time of the dogmatic definition, his own sermons on December 8. No doubt, her conception is immaculate . . . but how can one possibly say that *she is her own conception*? So he took the offensive.

"You are trying to fool me. Do you know what those words mean?"

Bernadette shook her head in sheer misery.

"Then how can you say a thing like this if you don't even understand it?"

9

"I kept repeating it all the way over here!" (René Laurentin; *Récit authentique des apparitions*, p. 225 and ff. Éd. Lethielleux)

Fr. G.M. Domanski, formerly International Director of the Militia of the Immaculata, wrote of Father Kolbe:

He went to Lourdes only once in his life, on January 30, 1930. He had come to beg Mary's blessing before leaving for his mission in the Far East. But the Servant of God had been closely connected with Lourdes ever since his youth, and not only because in 1914 his right thumb, which the doctors wanted to amputate, had been miraculously healed by an application of Lourdes water, thus making it possible for him to continue on to the priesthood. The ideal to which he devoted his entire life was based upon Mary's revelation of herself in her apparitions to Bernadette, to Sister Catherine Labouré (the Miraculous Medal), and to Alphonse Ratisbonne in Rome. *(Lourdes et le Pére Maximilien Kolbe: a sketch of his Mariology*, 2nd ed. Rome, 1974, Avant-Propos, p. 3)

As Mary Immaculate suggests by lifting her gaze heavenward, let us raise our own thoughts to God first of all, to God One in Three, in order to try to answer Father Kolbe's question: "Who then are you, O Immaculate Conception?"[3]

ENDNOTES

[1] In Polish: *Oswiecim*. In fact St. Maximilian Kolbe frequently spoke during his captivity. We have some accounts of his spiritual talks: one by M. Koscielniak and the other by Father Szweda; this latter tells us that he explained how the Immaculata is in the midst of the life of the Three Divine Persons.

[2] The Latin text runs: *Ergo non accidens aliquid, sed de natura Ejus. Illa Ipsa est Conceptio Immaculata.*

[3] It should be noted that the expression immaculate has here two related but different meanings. When we say that the Virgin was conceived immaculate, we mean that she was preserved, in time, from Original Sin, the sin she would have incurred as a daughter of Adam. But when used to designate a perfection of the divine life, as we shall see, this term immaculate is taken in a positive sense, even though it is negative in form. It is connected with those negative expressions that permit us to speak in a positive way of God. For instance we say that God is infinite, immense, immaterial, uncreated and so on. When we apply the term immaculate to God, we do so analogically in the sense that we give it when we speak of immaculate snow, for example. Snow is white in a positive way, without stain, for that is a property of its nature. In the same way, careful to preserve due proportion, we say God is immaculate: he is wholly light, wholly beauty, without shadow. The Virgin is immaculate because she was conceived through a denial of sin. For this reason she is, in a positive way, the Immaculate Conception; "it was inscribed in her very nature," says Father Kolbe, although it may be a divine Name, the Name of the third Divine Person, as we shall see with Saint Maximilian in the course of our study.

Chapter 2

AN IMMACULATE CONCEPTION
IN THE HOLY TRINITY

I T IS WORTH NOTING HOW, WHILE REMAINING FAITHFUL TO
the terminology of scholastic theology, Father Kolbe
shows himself a real apostle. We must not be deceived,
nor pay attention only to the outward expression of his thought.
His intuitions reach much deeper than might appear in the
technical language he knows as a Doctor of Theology, and
which he uses to make sure that he keeps strictly within the
limits of Catholic orthodoxy.

Here was the problem he faced. How can we discover in
God the principle which justifies Mary's astounding words:
"I am the Immaculate Conception"? Whenever we say in a
concrete way that a person *is* some abstract reality, we are saying what can only be said of God. Thus, Jesus says: "I am the
Way, the Truth, the Life." We say that God is perfect Goodness, Mercy, and so on. Since the Most Blessed Virgin cannot
as a creature *be* Conception, if she does choose to manifest
her personal identity by this term it must be because, with
reference to God, and in her humility as his handmaid, she
sees herself existing from all eternity in God's mind as the
Immaculate Conception.

Father Kolbe wants this examination of Mary's identity to be kept quite simple, since it must be of help to all Christians who desire to consecrate themselves to God through the Immaculata. Not, of course, that he hesitates to call upon the believer to exercise his intellect vigorously in considering the revelation which God has given us, through Jesus, of his own intimate life; only thus will we be able to grasp to some extent the secret meaning of this consecration.

So Father Kolbe ponders on the Trinity.

1. Who Is the Father?

As Jesus constantly repeated, and St. Paul after him, we give God the Father the name "God" in the absolute sense. Father Kolbe noted this:

> Our Lord is God, the unique God, infinite, infallible, thrice holy, all merciful. He, our Lord, our Father, our Creator, our End, is Intelligence, Power, Love, and all things. . . . Whatever is not God lacks all value apart from him. So then, all love, without limits, for our Father, the best of Fathers. . . . (Letter to his brother, April 21, 1919)

God the Father is the origin; he is the Unbegotten, the Principle that has no principle in the Godhead. He is also the End, the terminus to which everything returns.

> Ordinarily, everything comes from the Father through the Son and by the Holy Spirit; and everything returns by the Spirit through the Son to the Father. (Conference, June 20, 1937)

> There is only one Father in the Trinity, and as regards creatures: God the Father! What depths of meaning in our Lord's words: "Do not call anyone your father on earth" (Mt 23:9). Truly, no man can be a father in the full sense of that word; the primary principle of everything, the first

Father of all that exists, is God the Father. Everywhere else we find only an echo of his fatherhood. It is from the Father that all the divinity pours out, so to speak, from all eternity, on the Son; and from Father and Son on the Holy Spirit; and from the Blessed Trinity on the Virgin Mary, mother of Jesus, who is God. (Meditation, April 14, 1933)

The Father, then, is the Father because as such he eternally begets the Son. As regards the Holy Spirit the Father is also a principle, but without being his father.

Such precision in language is necessary, for if the first Person of the Trinity is the Father because he begets the Son, he is also, with the Son, the principle from which the Holy Spirit proceeds. But this third Person is not called a "*son*" of the Father because, as we shall see, he does not draw his origin from the Father by generation.

Of course, God speaks about himself in an analogous manner, using our human language, when he says of himself that he is Father, Son and Holy Spirit. We understand perfectly that he is not a father in the same sense that a man is when he transmits life to a son like himself. God is a pure spirit.

But there can be no father without a son. To understand a little better what divine generation implies, let us try to pinpoint what and who the Son is.

2. Who Is the Son?

Who is the Son? The Begotten One, because from the beginning and for all eternity he is begotten by the Father.

Even if we wish to transpose our human mode of speaking from the human level, where flesh and spirit are intertwined, to the supremely spiritual level where God operates (as Jesus does in the Gospel), we should keep in mind a few simple definitions such as the following:

To beget means to produce through generation; usually said of a male. If said of a woman, it means to conceive, to give birth to.

So much for the dictionary definition. Our Catholic faith does not hesitate to say that the Son is not only begotten, but also conceived and brought forth. Can there be in God, with regard to the Son, a Father who begets him and a mother by whom he is conceived and brought forth?

Can we admit that there is a "mother" in God, in the Holy Trinity?

The question has been asked by theologians. After having reminded us that "in the act of human generation it is the father who gives his specific nature to the child; but it is the mother who conceives it and gives it birth," St. Thomas concludes that it would be impossible to find in God a "maternal principle" of generation distinct from the paternal principle. For him, and in accordance with the notions current in his time, the mother's role in physical generation is "passive and receptive"; if this were projected into God there would be a certain *inequality* between the paternal and the maternal principle, which is impossible. The saint does, however, go on to draw a very interesting conclusion from all this: "The acts that distinguish the father from the mother in physical generation are both attributed to the father alone in the generation of the Word, according to Scripture, for it says that the Father gives life to the Son (Jn 5:26), and also that he conceives the Word and brings him forth" (*Summa contra* G. IV. Ch. 11, end).

This argument is perfectly valid today; for even if we admit that in physical generation father and mother are really co-principles of new life, there still exists definite interdependence between them. This is something that we cannot admit among the divine Persons. How could we imagine that in God there could be two Persons who would need to complete each other's activity in order to bring it to perfection?

16

So Father Kolbe states that:

> From all eternity the Father begets the Son, without a mother. (Notes, 1939)

Let us then hold firm on this point: the Son is begotten, conceived and brought forth by the Father alone, *as the Son*. He is related to the Father as the Begotten to the Begetter.

Then what is the role of the Holy Spirit in the Trinity, since everything the Father possesses the Son likewise possesses in perfect unity of nature with the Father? What is left that they can exchange? God is love; hence it is in love that the Son is begotten, conceived, brought forth. He is distinct from the Father even though he is brought forth in "the bosom of the Father" (Jn 1:18).

Human intelligence by itself is incapable of penetrating these intimate secrets of God's own trinitarian being. These secrets were revealed by Jesus Christ:

> I tell you the truth: it is expedient for you that I go; for if I go not, the Paraclete will not come to you; but if I go, I will send him to you. And when he is come, the Spirit of truth, he will teach you all truth. For he shall not speak of himself, but what things soever he shall hear, he shall speak; and the things that are to come he shall show you. He shall glorify me, because he shall receive of mine, and shall show it to you. (Jn 16:7, 13-14)

The Son cannot be known except through the Holy Spirit whom the Son is to send us:

> Before Christ, the mystery of the Blessed Trinity was scarcely known or hinted at. For the world to know it, the second Person of the Blessed Trinity became a man, and lived in this world; this was the first step towards a perfect knowledge of God. But for the Son to be more truly known, the Holy Spirit, the third Person of the Holy Trinity, had to come to us. (Conference, September 25, 1937)

17

3. Who is the Holy Spirit?

Let us re-read what Father Kolbe says in his last writing, his spiritual testament; never before had he expressed so clearly his thinking about the third Person of the Trinity:

> And who is the Holy Spirit? The flowering of the love of the Father and the Son. If the fruit of created love is a created conception, then the fruit of divine Love, that prototype of all created love, is necessarily a divine "conception." The Holy Spirit is, therefore, the "uncreated eternal conception," the prototype of all the conceptions that multiply life throughout the whole universe.
>
> The Father begets; the Son is begotten; the Spirit is the "conception" that springs from their love; there we have the intimate life of the three Persons by which they can be distinguished one from another. But they are united in the oneness of their nature, of their divine existence. The Spirit is, then, this thrice holy "conception," this infinitely holy "immaculate conception."

In this passage Father Kolbe shows himself a truly original thinker; he is perhaps the first to have intuited that the Holy Spirit is the "uncreated conception" in God.

However, a difficulty arises here. Would this expression not fit the Son more properly, since he is indeed "conceived" by the Father alone? Since the divine generation of the Son takes place in the depths of God's being, "in the bosom of the Father" (Jn 1:18), the term "conception" seems to be the most correct one we can use in speaking of this divine act of generation: the Father begets him by conceiving him without any intermediary. As St. Thomas observed, the Father alone is at once the Father and the "mother" of the Word, his Son.

The Holy Spirit: a Divine Maternity of Love

Since God reveals himself to us by employing human realities that we are familiar with, let us look again for a moment at the mother's role. So far we have been considering, in the act of generation, only the physical, carnal relationships which are common to man and to the higher animals. But what distinguishes man from beast is spirit. In conceiving and bringing forth her child, and in all that follows its birth, a mother has a role that is totally peculiar to her, a role destined for her by nature itself.

As Father Lemonnyer says so correctly, seeking to pinpoint the "maternal role of the Holy Spirit in our supernatural life":

> It is indeed a mother's task, and one of the most sacred, to help the child to get to know its father. What concern she shows, what efforts she makes, to succeed in this task! *"Incipe, parve puer, risu cognoscere PATREM!"* ("Begin, little one, to recognize your father by smiling at him!"). What joy fills the mother's heart when she sees the baby greet its father by waving its tiny arms and smiling! What joy, especially, when for the first time the child manages to shape his baby lips into the word "Daddy"—a truly sacred word she has been trying so long to get him to utter.

I know a young mother who told me once, with surprise, "My baby said *Daddy* even before he said *Mamma*." I congratulated her for having succeeded so well in fulfilling her role as a mother. For by talking so much about Daddy while he was absent at work, and by forgetting herself, this mother had helped bring about the true spiritual birth of her child. He had come forth from her womb physically, at birth; along with her husband she had begotten him; now he was beginning to enter upon a new life in the depths of his father's heart, thanks to the love in his mother's breast. This marvel took place because the father was hoping for and expecting this new degree of fatherhood, this recognition from his child, under the inspiration of his wife—a fruit of the love they had pledged to each other the day they were engaged. It is thus that in truly happy families the mother's heart is the bond of mutual and fruitful love between father and children.

So Father Kolbe was perfectly right when he said:

And who is the Holy Spirit? He is the flowering of the love of the Father and the Son.

St. Thomas had expressed the same truth using a similar image. The Holy Spirit, he says, "is like the flower which shows that the tree is healthy" (*STI* q. 37). For Father Kolbe, the Holy Spirit is like the flower or the fruit which reveals how living and productive is the love between the Persons of the Blessed Trinity.

As regards creatures, God shows both a fatherly and a motherly love. Here is what an excellent contemporary exegete has to say on this point[1]:

The prophets compare the love of God sometimes to a father's love, sometimes to that of a mother. Both kinds of love have their primary source in God, and in him alone. According to Scripture, we find in God, a type of tenderness which is not only fatherly, but motherly. It was this that brought forth the marvellous masterpiece of all creation, the heart of a mother. This is the same tenderness that our contemporary world, hard and inhuman as it is, busily engaged in committing one mortal error after another, like a badly brought-up child, so desperately needs to re-discover in order to find salvation. Further on we shall show that the world needs to turn to Mary's intercession, to woman's special role, in order to attain this salvation; and it will do this provided women come to realize what their specific Christian vocation is.

Are there anywhere in the Bible passages more poignantly moving than those in which God's love for man whom he wishes to save is likened to a mother's love? For example:

"As nurslings you shall be carried in her arms, and fondled in her lap; as a mother comforts her son, so will I comfort you" (Is 66:12-13). "Sion said: The Lord has forsaken me; my Lord has forgotten me. Can a mother forget her infant, or be without tenderness for the child of her womb? Even should she forget, I will never forget you!" (Is 49:14-15) Even a mother's heart, then, is only an image of God's motherly love. Does not Sirach promise: "God will love you more than your mothers did?" (Eccl 4:10) Isaiah says (46:3-4) that Yahweh has never ceased bearing Israel in his arms like a mother (cf. Nm 11:12-14); and Osee declares (11:3-4) that God has taught Israel to walk, even as a mother teaches her child. The author of Psalm 131 (v. 2) tells us that he kept his soul quiet and peaceful in God's presence, just as a little child does, enfolded in his mother's embrace. In several places the Bible tells of men seeking refuge in God like young birds beneath their mother's wings. (Ru 2:12, Ps 57:2; 61:5; 91:4)

After demonstrating that it is the human couple, male and female, fully completing each other, which bears the "image and resemblance" of God, Father Feuillet concludes:

Taking into consideration these Biblical viewpoints, one can realize—even though this is not stated in so many words—that Adam who names all the creatures in the universe, establishes his dominion over them, and organizes them, is more particularly the reflection of the divine Logos, the Word or Son; whereas the woman, Eve, who brings forth new life and plays such an intimate role in the mysterious budding forth of life and in its development is nearer to the Spirit, the Principle of all life.

The Hebrew word for spirit, "*ruah*" is feminine. No doubt, the one God of Israel admits of no subaltern "god" or "goddess;" and the Holy Spirit is certainly not some

21

sort of female divinity. . . . The mystery of woman is essentially interior; and by it she approaches the "interiorness" of the mystery of God's own Spirit. If woman makes man know himself more fully, the Holy Spirit, on his side, as St. Paul says, is the one who makes Christians conscious of their dignity as children of God. "For the Spirit bears witness to our spirit, that we are the children of God" (Rom 8:16). Further on, we shall apply these notions to the role of the Most Blessed Virgin Mary, and of women in general, to the whole economy of Christianity.

We thought it worthwhile to quote rather extensively the words of this author, in order to highlight the way in which Father Kolbe's intuitions coincide with the considered scientific conclusions of a highly qualified exegete. In God there is no "mother," no spouse of the Father, who collaborates with him in the ineffable generation of the Word.

The Father begets the Son without any mother. (Notes, 1933)

So affirms Father Kolbe. But if God is the Father because he begets his Son, he also conceives his "first born of every creature" with the tenderness of a mother, and experiences a thrill of love in contemplating this Son, the "splendor of his own substance." The Son's response of love as he bursts forth from the depths of the Father's bosom (cf. Jn 1:18), reveals the maternal role of the Holy Spirit infinitely better than the word "Daddy" on a child's lips discloses the love in his mother's heart.

In God, in the very depths of the divine being, there exists a certain motherhood of love, the Holy Spirit, who links Father and Son with each other in joy and peace.

Basing ourselves on these analogies taken from human life, we can begin to understand something of this maternal love found in God.

A human mother is an image of our Heavenly Mother (the Immaculata), and she in turn is the image of God's own goodness, God's own heart. God's perfections, flowing from the ineffable inner life of the Trinity, repeat themselves throughout creation in numberless forms, like so many echoes. Thus it is that, starting out from creatures, our heart can rise even to the knowledge and the love of God in the Blessed Trinity; but our heart also loves these created forms because they do come from God, are created by him, and belong entirely to him. (Letter to his mother, December 8, 1932)

The Holy Spirit, Divine Gift
Bestowed by the Father and the Son

As Father Lemonnyer writes:

There is undoubtedly close affinity between the personal properties characterizing the Holy Spirit, and those that characterize a mother. Of the three divine Persons, he is the One who is "given" to us in a very special way. He is the Gift of God "*par excellence*"; it is a name he reserves for himself. In the Trinity itself, he is Love personified; this too is one of the names proper to him. But to whom, more than to a mother, do these two qualifications belong? Do they not define her? No other person on earth is "given" to us as our mother is; no one else so well as she personifies love in its most disinterested, generous and devoted aspects. (*ibid*. p. 244)

If the Spirit is the Gift of God, he is also the source of all gifts, in the depths of the Trinity's own life, and in all life outside of God. We would never have dreamed of the existence of this Third Person; and if Christ had not revealed it to us we would never have known that the Spirit is God's Love and God's Gift. Now, however, that this revelation has been made, and that the Holy Spirit has manifested himself, we can no longer consider the Father and the Son apart from their relationship with the Holy Spirit, their common Love, springing forth from the bosom of the Trinity, the perfect Gift of self.

Self-giving; self-forgetfulness. It is worth remarking how the Holy Spirit, filled with the bliss of giving himself to the Father through the Son, is like a silent witness to the intimacy of their mutual love. In the discourse after the Last Supper, when Jesus had revealed the third divine Person as the Spirit of truth and love (Jn 14-16), he addressed himself to his Father in prayer, moved by this same Spirit, and asked him to make known to the disciples and to us through them the intimacy of the life he lives with the Father, a life which he sums up in these words: "Father, you are in me, and I in you" (Jn 17- 21). The Holy Spirit is not mentioned at all in this Chapter 17, yet without the Holy Spirit, divine life is not possible; without him God is no longer God. When we come to understand (to glimpse, rather), the maternal role played by the Spirit in the bosom of the Trinity, we can be sure that he was actively present in Jesus' sacerdotal prayer. Like any mother, he is a Gift both for the Father and the Son, and Gift for us too, even as he is for them. "I have *given* them the glory which you gave to me, so that they may be one, as we are one; I in them and you in me, so that they may be made perfectly one" (v. 22-23). In God who is love, the Holy Spirit is the very glory of this love, the source of every gift, himself the pure gift of himself; in the "bosom of the Father" he is born as subtantial Love.

Can this Holy Spirit, God's maternal love, the Gift-of-himself because he is the Gift of the God of love, also be called, as Father Kolbe thought, the *uncreated Immaculate Conception*?

As we shall see, he considered "conception" very differently in his "testament" (given above) and in his sketch of 1940 [*see page 172*]. He goes beyond the analogy of "conception" drawn from the facts of physical generation. It is in the very life of

God the creator that he examines this question, considering it (after the example of St. Thomas in *STI* q. 44-45), in the light of the analogy with an artist who "conceives" and "creates" his masterpiece.

The Holy Spirit: Divine Conception of Love

In the spiritual order the word "to conceive" refers primarily to "the act by which the mind apprehends and formulates an idea or design." By extension one might say that a "conception" or concept is a "creation of the mind," as when one would remark of something: "this is one of the noblest concepts of the human spirit" (Littré).

Think for a moment of Michelangelo's "Moses." This masterpiece, which is so universally admired, was, first of all, "conceived" in the artist's mind. He conceived a notion of the prophet in the Bible, and "saw" Moses in so real and impressive a manner that, once he had translated his ideal into marble, he suffered because he did not find in the statue the life which the image possessed in his own mind. "Speak!" he cried, hurling the chisel in his hand at the head of the marble personage he had created. Michelangelo learned then that he was not really a creator. His mind, rich and prolific though it was, could not really achieve fatherhood. With all the love inspired by the vision of the living image of Moses which his mind had spiritually conceived, he threw himself enthusiastically into the task of creating, outside of himself, this marble projection of his vision, to make of it an external expression of his inner spiritual concept of Moses. So, he went to the quarries, selected a certain block of marble, and with his usual genius set about carving it; and with this material thus chosen he succeeded in making the masterpiece which did indeed correspond to his inner vision. But not being able to confer life on his creation, he understood that in its regard he was neither a true creator nor a true father.

This example helps us to understand that a conception is the fruit of the soul: of intelligence and will, no doubt; but it is above all an idea, a mental word spoken by the intellect. If we wish to glimpse the divine mystery of the uncreated conception, we need to realize that the Word of God fulfills in all its plenitude his title of Son, and that he is the perfect conception testifying the fatherhood of God, who sees himself and expresses himself as he really is, in the person of this Son.

However, Father Kolbe is thinking of the Holy Spirit, not of the Son, when he speaks of the "uncreated conception" in the Blessed Trinity. What can we make of this notion?

In its spiritual sense, the word "to conceive" has a number of meanings, especially two. First of all, "to form a concept, a general idea." This is an act of the intellect. Using this analogy, we may say that the Son is begotten or conceived by the Father; he is so to speak the terminus of the act of knowing, in which a mind expresses itself in a word, the outward projection of an inner idea.

But there is also another meaning of the word "to conceive": "to begin to experience a sentiment, a passion" as when one says, "I conceived a deep affection for him."

"My soul has its secret, my life has its mystery—an eternal love in a moment conceived" (Arvers).

In this latter meaning the word "to conceive" belongs to the area of the will, to the affective sphere rather than that of the intellect. To experience love for someone, or to experience a feeling of friendship and affection for him is, by analogy, what happens in the life of the Trinity between the Father and his beloved Son. In God's eternal NOW—for this is the only correct way of speaking about God's being, which knows neither after nor before—in which the Son is begotten or conceived as God's Word, the Holy Spirit is that Love which bursts forth from God, the pressure of Love, the flame of Love, that the Father has for the Son and the Son for the Father. Thus one may say that the Father and the Son "conceive" each for the other a Love which is, then, Love's very conception. Even as the Son is the Word that the Father speaks, so too the Holy Spirit is the Father's conception through the Son, or rather he is the conception of each of them.

For everything comes forth from the Father, and returns to the Father. Father Kolbe writes:

All graces come from the Father through the Son and by the Holy Spirit (Conference, Sept. 25, 1937). Normally, everything comes from the Father through the Son and by the Holy Spirit; and everything goes back to the Father by the Holy Spirit through the Son. (Conference, June 20, 1937)

In the order of love the Father is the primary principle and the last end. The Father is rapt in love, and conceives by the Love he has for his Son simultaneously as he begets him. And the Son is rapt in Love, and conceives by the Love he has for his Father simultaneously as he is begotten. So it is that Father and Son each conceive by their reciprocal love; this is why the Holy Spirit can be termed the conception springing from Love, as Father Kolbe so formally puts it.

This manner of considering the life of love in the bosom of the Trinity brings us back to the images employed by the Fathers of the Church—for instance the one utilized by St. Ireneus: "In truth, it is the Father who anoints the Son, and it is the Son who is anointed in the Spirit, who is the Unction."[2]

Unction; Conception; both are names used properly of the Holy Spirit. We can say, therefore, that the Father conceives by love for his Son, who conceives by love for his Father in the Holy Spirit, the uncreated Conception of divine Love. Father Kolbe is right in saying that the Holy Spirit is the Immaculate Conception (in the positive meaning of essential purity), the "uncreated Immaculate Conception."

Although we can *distinguish* these two sorts of "conception"—of thought and of love—we must above all avoid separating them, but rather try to understand their *union*.

Why did Michelangelo "conceive" such a deep love for his "Moses"? Certainly because he had "conceived" such an exalted idea of the prophet, such a beautiful and attractive image, that he felt a flame of love for it welling up in his heart. But at the same time, this "conception" of his would not have been so attractive, would not have provoked such a movement of love if he had not experienced towards it a sort of *a priori* affection. True, we love only what we know; but it is also true that we get to know intimately only what we love; and no one would try to know more deeply if he did not already *desire* to know, if he did not wish to formulate clearly in his mind a "word" which would express more adequately the thing he already loved so much.

Every mother provides an illustration of this truth. No doubt she wants to know her child better and better, so as to educate him according to his real needs. Yet there is behind all this a sort of *a priori* love at the bottom of her knowledge, a love that furnishes her with a notion, a "concept" of her child which stirs her heart. Even though the child's defects outweigh his qualities, he will always be surrounded, penetrated by the love of his mother, who would like to see him reborn, made over in the image of what he ought to be as a true man; and if the mother is a Christian mother, in the image of what he ought to be as a child of God. Monica gave birth to Augustine twice: once in the flesh, and again through her tears. Her mother's love, so sorely tried by her son's disorderly life, brought Augustine to his new birth as a true and perfect Christian.

Similarly, but in infinitely higher degree, we should find in God who is Truth and Love a similar unity between the relationships that constitute the divine Persons. If the Father and the Son conceive through perfect love for each other—"This is my beloved Son; listen to him!" "I love the Father!"—it is because God the Father, when he conceives "the perfect image and splendor of his own substance" cannot fail subsequently to be moved to a conception springing from Love. But at the same time there is in God a sort of *a priori* love—for God is Love—which compels the Father so to speak to utter his Word, to envelop him and penetrate him with Love, thus enabling him also to be, as the Word, the source of this Love which is the Holy Spirit.

When we are thinking about these "conceptions" of thought and of love in God, it is normal that we examine them one after the other, i.e. that we speak of the Holy Spirit after speaking of the Word. But in the oneness of life that belongs to the three Persons, the conception of love envelops the conception by thought; and it is the Holy Spirit that urges the Son to cry out, "Abba, Father!"

> God is love; that is the Holy Trinity. The ebbing and flowing of love is what constitutes the life found in the bosom of the Trinity. (Sketch, 1940)

It was under this aspect of union—*reaction, return, reflux*—which were the usual similies he used, that Father Kolbe liked to consider the affirmation made by Mary at Lourdes. United as she was to the Holy Spirit, all her love was poured out on the Father through the Son, who was also *her* Son.

How can we grasp this profound, living union between Mary Immaculate and the Holy Spirit?

If it is true that the Holy Spirit is, in the bosom of the eternal and indivisible Trinity the spotless "Immaculate Conception," the Gift that the Father and the Son give to each other, the breath of love that binds them to one another, it would be logical to conclude that Mary's statement at Lourdes amounted to saying: "I am the Holy Spirit!"

However, let us be more realistic. Such an affirmation would contradict the very mystery of Mary herself. For she is a creature; immaculate though she is, she remains a mere human person, like each of us, and this even in the presence of the Trinity itself, where she is eternally glorified, in body, and in soul.

Mary, the humble Virgin, was "filled by the Holy Spirit" even from the time of her own conception in the womb of St. Anne her mother (cf. *Lumen Gentium*, n. 56). She is bathed, plunged into the Spirit of the Father and the Son to such an extent that when she says, "I am the Immaculate Conception" she means, "I am the manifestation, the *epiphany*, of the Holy Spirit." Beyond this we could even say that Mary is a true *theophany*,[3] a visible manifestation of the Father's infinite love for men, that love which, through the Holy Spirit, accomplishes in the Church the work of the redemption, the mission of the Son, who is also the Son of Mary. Is this not what Father Kolbe has in mind when he says:

> Mary Immaculate is the incarnation of divine mercy? (Conference, Nov. 24, 1938)

To answer this question with more certainty, let us consider with him the action of the *uncreated Immaculate Conception*, the Holy Spirit in Mary herself.

ENDNOTES

[1] A. Feuillet, *Jésus et sa Mére* (d'après les récits lucaniens de l'enfance et d'après S. Jean), Paris, Gabalda, 1974.

[2] H.M. Manteau-Bonamy, *La Vierge et le Saint-Esprit*, P. Lethielleux, 1971, p. 43, note 10.

[3] The term "theophany" is reserved in biblical language for "every manifestation of God perceptible to the senses" (*Dictionaire de la Foi chretienne* T.I., Cerf, 1968). The perceptible signs of God's presence in the Exodus of the Jews were theophanies as well as the signs attesting the presence of the Holy Spirit on the Pentecost in the Acts of the Apostles. Mary is the Theophany *par excellence*. We will see this with Father Kolbe.

Chapter 3

THE IMMACULATE CONCEPTION IN MARY

B EFORE STARTING TO CONSIDER WHAT MAKES MARY THE Immaculate Conception, it is good to stress, as Father Kolbe did, that these distinctions we make, and which our intellect needs in order to see more clearly and to understand better the reasons why we should love, must not turn into occasions of diversion and distraction in our life of worship.

Our imagination leads us to think of God the Father, of Jesus, of the Immaculata, as the objects of "devotions" which are more or less similar. Instead, we should think of them as links in a single chain, as elements all leading to a single goal: God, who is One in his Trinity. (Letter to Niepokalanow, November 10, 1934)

He insists on this idea:

Day by day, let us strive to belong more and more to the Immaculata, and in her and through her, to Jesus and to God; never should we try to go to Jesus without her. We do not serve God the Father, and Jesus our Lord, and the Immaculata; but we seek to serve God in Jesus and through Jesus, and to serve Jesus in the Immaculata and through the Immaculata. (Letter to Fr. Salezy Mikolajczyk, July 28, 1935)

Whenever we examine the relationships between Mary and God, we must always keep in mind these affirmations which put into proper perspective the trends of Father Kolbe's thought. The Virgin Mary occupies the central position in the effort of doctrinal reflection carried on by this great apostle of Mary. The formal veneration of Mary the Immaculata absorbs all his attention. Still, he has not failed to place her in her correct position, which is that of a creature, even if the position she occupies is the noblest of all; for she is Mary, the Mother of God and our Mother.

> No one should disapprove, [says Paul VI] . . . if Blessed Maximilian and the Church together with him show such enthusiasm for the formal veneration of the most Blessed Virgin; this enthusiasm will never be too great considering the merits and the advantages we can derive from such veneration, precisely because a mysterious communion unites Mary to Christ, a communion that is documented convincingly in the New Testament. Never let us think of this as "Mariolatry"; we know that the sun will never be dimmed by the light of the moon; and never will the ministry of salvation entrusted to the Church's solicitude in particular be impaired, if the Church is faithful to honor in Mary her most exceptional Daughter, and her spiritual Mother. (Beatification homily, October 17, 1971)

1. The Immaculata Is a Creature

The Mother of God is a creature. It follows that all she is, she has from God. But she is God's most perfect creature.

For this reason, the homage paid to her is, by the very nature of the case, paid to God himself. If we admire a statue, we honor the artist who created this masterpiece If we honor Mary most holy we honor God. The more we pay homage to the divine perfections found in Mary, the more perfect is our homage to God; this is perfectly in order, since God created her in the highest state of perfection. (Conference, April 9, 1938)

Why do we love Mary Immaculate and consecrate ourselves to her unreservedly? Not because of what she is in herself, but because she is wholly God's . . . We love her because we love God. (Conference, April 4, 1938)

Michelangelo produced a masterpiece, no doubt; but his "Moses" did not completely satisfy him, for he knew how far the realization fell short of his inner ideal. True, his "Moses" done in marble revealed the wealth of the artist's spiritual conception, which was in him all light and love. A true masterpiece is a work in which the artist—because he possesses the genius to do it—is able to transpose his inner conceptions into marble, or onto canvas, or into music.

But he cannot, of course, confer on his creation the kind of existence it has in his own mind; it remains only a symbol of the inner, ideal conception; and like any other symbol it remains distinct from what it symbolizes. A flag is not the same thing as the country it stands for.

In terms of human procreation, human parents know perfectly well that they cannot produce the spiritual soul of their child, even though they have already "conceived" him in their minds. That is why we call their action "*pro*creation;" in this process of human generation God himself immediately creates the spirit and soul of man. God alone is the wonderful artist who is able to create a being in his own "image and likeness."

What does this mean?

Father Kolbe explains very precisely how a creature must go back to the principle from which it sprang, in order to achieve the complete fullness of being that the Creator intended it to reach:

Everywhere in this world we notice action and the reaction which is equal but contrary to it; we find departure

35

and return, going away and coming back, separation and reunion. The separation always looks forward to union, which is creative. All this is simply an image of the Blessed Trinity in the activity of creatures. Union means love, creative love. Divine activity, outside the Trinity itself, follows a like pattern. First God creates the universe: that is something like a separation. Creatures, by following the natural law given to them by God, reach their perfection, become like him, and go back to him. Intelligent creatures love him in a conscious manner; through this love they unite themselves more and more closely with him, and so find their way back to him.

The creature most completely filled with this love, filled with God himself, is the Immaculata, who never contracted the slightest stain of sin, who never departed in the least from God's will. United to the Holy Spirit as his spouse, in an ineffable manner, she is one with God in an incomparably more perfect way than can be predicated of any other creature.

It is from this point of view—of action and reaction, of flux and reflux—that Father Kolbe considers the relationships between God and the Immaculata, between the Creator and his creatures, even the noblest of them all, the Virgin Mary. He had borrowed this notion from the field of natural science, in which he had achieved a certain competence.

Everywhere in nature we observe the phenomenon of action and reaction. This is a reflection of the activity of the Blessed Trinity itself. [In the relationships between God and creatures, we might say that] "the action is God's, who creates from nothing; the reaction is that of creatures insofar as they tend toward and return to their Creator, more or less perfectly." (Conference, June 27, 1936)

He makes himself clearer and broadens his idea to take in the domain of grace, before he turns his consideration toward the most excellent of all creatures, the Immaculata.

> We know by divine revelation that from all eternity the Father begets the Son, and that the Holy Spirit proceeds from the Father and the Son. This inner life of the Trinity repeats and re-echoes itself in innumerable and varied ways in the creatures that have come forth from the hand of God, who is One in his Holy Trinity, as more or less distant images of him. The universal principle which holds that every effect must have some likeness to its cause, applies here all the more fully and exactly because God creates out of nothing; nothing exists in all creation that he has not made.

> Now, every act of God's love comes down from the Father through the Son and by the Holy Spirit, creating, sustaining, giving life and growth in the natural order as well as in that of grace. This is how God pours out his love on the numberless limited resemblances of himself that he has made. And the reaction of love on the part of the creature must follow the selfsame path in order to go back to the Father: by the Holy Spirit and through the Son. We may not always realize this, but so it is. The act of love in the creature has no other author but God himself; still, when the creature is intelligent and free, this act of love cannot happen without its consent. (Sketch, 1940)

Father Kolbe thus takes his place in the ranks of those mighty Christian thinkers, who like to consider in this way the whole cycle of life: in God first of all, and then in creatures which come from God. It is interesting to see this apostolic man, so much at home with the humblest folk, and so adept at leading them to God, not hesitating to address them in language similar to that used by the Doctors of the Church. Note how closely his teaching follows that of these great saints.

37

Issuing from the Primary Principle, creatures accomplish a sort of circuit, a gyratory movement, such that all things when they tend to their proper end, are returning to the Principle whence they came forth. It is to be expected therefore that this return to their proper end should be brought about by the same causes which effected their going forth from the source. Now we know that the order of the origin of the divine Persons is the supreme reason for the production of creatures by the Primary Principle; it must then be the reason for their return to their end. We were created by the Son and by the Holy Spirit; and hence it is by them that we are brought back to our end. Such was the idea expressed by St. Augustine when he spoke of the Principle (the Father) to which we are returning, of the Model (the Son) that we must follow, and of the Grace which reconciles us with God (the Holy Spirit). Such was also the concept of St. Hilary. (St. Thomas, in *The Book of Sentences*, I, dist. 14, q. 2 a.2)

St. Ireneus had said something very similar. Thus, the master theologians speak the same language as the zealous apostle—a language that can be grasped by all, even simple people. It is not difficult, in fact, to consider these various movements of action and reaction, of falling and rising, of going forth and coming back, of flux and reflux, so as to find in them a precise *image* on which faith can find footing when it seeks to penetrate the ineffable mystery of the God who reveals himself to us. That image has the same pedagogical value as those used by Jesus in his parables, to lead us to the unspeakable truths about God he was trying to inculcate.

As early as 1938 Father Kolbe had outlined his main thoughts on the unique place occupied by the Immaculata in the story of salvation. In the first lines, he mentions this favorite comparison of his: action and reaction, with its starting point and its point of final return in God the Father, so as to show that in this return current the Holy Spirit is the moving principle, just as in the going forth he is the *terminus ad quem.*

In 1939, in another sketch developing this same theme he did not hesitate to write:

> Every action has the reaction in view. The reaction is the fruit of the action. God the Father is the primary Principle and the Last End. The Immaculata is full of grace; nothing in the way of grace is lacking to her. The path of grace is always the same: action: from the Father through the Son (Christ said, "I will send him to you"), and by the Holy Spirit (the Immaculata); then the inverse reaction: from creatures through the Immaculata (the Holy Spirit), and Christ (the Word) back to the Father. Action and reaction=love=grace and good works. (Notes, 1939)

He finds the Virgin Mary, the Immaculate one, therefore at the *end* of the *action* we see in the life of the Trinity, which passes from the Father through the Word to the Holy Spirit; and he finds her at the *starting point* of the *reaction* in which we see divine life flowing back from the Holy Spirit through the Incarnate Word to the Father.

Mary, *in se*, is neither the end nor the starting point; but it should be emphasized that she is present *at* the end and *at* the beginning or starting point by reason of her tremendously intimate union with the Holy Spirit.

To help us understand—to get some faint idea, rather—of this deep union between the Holy Spirit and the Immaculata, he compares it to the union between Christ's humanity and the Person of the Word. If we follow him in what he says, we shall see that it is rich in insights which throw light on the true place Mary occupies: that of God's "first born daughter." His words are perfectly measured, for he never forgets that Mary is only a creature:

The Immaculata comes forth from the Father, through the Son and the Holy Spirit, as from her Creator who calls all creatures out of nothing to existence—in the very image of the Trinity—because he loves to find in them the image of himself that they bear. Creatures endowed with reason and will know and recognize that they come from God and receive all from him, i.e. what they are, what they can do, what they possess moment by moment. (Sketch, 1940)

2. The Union of the Divine and the Human in Mary

To avoid any possible misunderstanding, let us state it clearly at the outset: Christ is the incarnate Word of God, God made man. The Immaculate Virgin is not an incarnation of the Holy Spirit; she is a pure human creature, a descendant of Adam. Father Kolbe repeats this untiringly.

If he likes to compare the union of the divine and the human in Christ, on the one hand, and in Mary on the other, he is careful to point out the essential differences that characterize the two cases.

The Holy Spirit is in Mary after the fashion, one might say, in which the Second Person of the Blessed Trinity, the Word, is in his humanity. There is, of course, this difference: in Jesus there are two natures, divine and human, but one single person who is God. Mary's nature and person are totally distinct from the nature and person of the Holy Spirit. Still, their union is inexpressible, and so perfect that the Holy Spirit acts only by the Immaculata, his spouse. . . . (Letter to Fr. Salezy Mikolajczyk, July 28, 1935)

If we wish to avoid error when speaking of the mystery of Christ we must affirm both of the following propositions: a) The man Christ never began *to be*; and b) Christ did begin *to be a man* (cf. St. Thomas, *ST III*, q. 16, a. 9; ad 3). In these two propositions which, we repeat, we must never separate but rather consider together, we have the expression of the mystery of God's Son become man. In Jesus Christ the divine and the human are joined so closely that there is one single being, the Son of the Eternal Father, who is God even as the Father and the Holy Spirit are. Our difficulty in understanding this arises no doubt from the mystery itself; but also from the fact that we are not capable of defining with rigorous precision what we mean by the word "being."

Either a "being" means "one who is, who exists"; and then it is true to say that the man Christ never began to exist ("Before Abraham was, I am" [Jn 8:58]). Here he speaks as God, even in his human form; "I am who am." He shows that he exists as a divine Person, even when he is acting in a human manner.

Or again, "to be" may mean to exist in some determined manner: one can be here or there, one can be great or small, one can be a man, be intelligent, be alive . . . In this sense one must say that Jesus began to be a man, i.e. began to exist as a man. The Second Person of the Trinity, on becoming incarnate, began to be a human being, because he had determined that he would become one of us, starting from his conception in a woman's womb. Still, even though he had become a man he never ceased to be the eternal "I am." This is why Father Kolbe is careful to express the dogma correctly:

> "In Jesus there are two natures, the divine and the human, but only one Person, who is God."

How then can we speak of a similar union between Mary the Immaculata and the Holy Spirit? Father Kolbe never forgets that it was Mary herself who stressed this union when she said at Lourdes: "I am the Immaculate Conception."

In contrast with the mystery of the hypostatic union in Christ, the words "I am" do not here indicate divine existence but the concrete existence of a human person, born of Adam's race, just like every other daughter of humankind. What she said to Bernadette was: "I, who speak to you, whom you see as a woman, as a member of your own race, am the Immaculate Conception."

She is really and truly a human person, who began to exist in time, like every other individual of our race; but at the same time the name she uses reminds us of the names proper to the Holy Spirit.

Should we perhaps conclude that Mary has *become* the Holy Spirit? Certainly not! for she is and remains a pure creature. But we should say that this young woman of our race *has never existed apart from the Holy Spirit*, who is the Immaculate Conception in God. In more or less the same way St. Paul wrote: "I am crucified with Christ; and if I live, it is no longer I who live, it is Christ who lives in me" (Gal 2:19-20). Through his Spirit Christ had taken over all the vital energies of Paul, his ardent apostle, to such an extent that the latter really lived with Christ's own life. In how much more sublime a way did not the Spirit of Christ take possession of the entire life of this daughter of Adam, from the very first moment of her existence, to make of her the Mother of Christ? Her life was then nothing but the life given her by the Spirit of the Father and of the Son.

A marvelous mystery lies hidden here: the mystery of the presence of a divine Person in a creature taken up so totally, down to the very roots of her being, into his control, and for all time. But like every other mystery, this one too is an overabundance of light, which stimulates the weak intelligence of the believer, and will not let it rest.

If the spirit of evil is capable of "possessing" a human creature to the point of identifying the latter with itself, even in a sort of personal way (see Mt 8:29, Mk 1:23-25, Lk 8:28-30), then surely *a fortiori* the Spirit of God can take possession of his privileged creature, Mary. The evil spirit *enslaves* the poor creature which he takes over, whereas the Holy Spirit *stirs up and strengthens liberty* deep in the soul of the one in whom he deigns to dwell. Better than anyone else, Mary reveals the presence of the Holy Spirit in her *by all she is*, by her words, her actions, her whole life. And under this impulse of the Holy Spirit Mary declared: "I am the Immaculate Conception."

For this reason Father Kolbe does not hesitate to say:

Jesus Christ has two natures, divine and human, which are united in one single divine Person; such is the exact and precise formulation of the dogma. The Immaculata is united to the Holy Spirit so closely that we really cannot grasp this union. But we can at least say that the Holy Spirit and Mary are two persons who live in such intimate union that they have but one sole life. (Conference, June 27, 1936)

Such a daring affirmation is merely the echo of a no less surprising one which we find in Pius IX's Bull *Ineffabilis Deus*, defining the dogma of Mary's Immaculate Conception.

Even before the Virgin Mother of God was conceived by Anne, her mother, it was necessary that grace should have been at work and produced its fruit; it was necessary that she who was to conceive the "first-born of every creature" should herself have been conceived as God's first-born daughter.

Of course, we are not using the word "before" in a purely temporal sense here, as though the Most Blessed Virgin had existed corporally prior to her conception in the flesh! But at the very instant in which she was physically conceived, this child *was*; she *existed* in God as his first-born daughter, divinely conceived by the Holy Spirit.

Hence, from the moment of her physical conception she is already defined as the Immaculate Conception, because she lives only under the intimate and vital action of the Holy Spirit, the divine Conception of Love.

Vatican II says the same thing in different words:

The Mother of God, the all-holy Mary, was preserved from

43

every stain of sin, for she had been formed by the Holy Spirit as a new creature. (*Lumen Gentium*, n. 56)

The fifth century heresiarch, Nestorius, tried to imagine what sort of union joined the Son of God and the man Jesus. He maintained that the Person of the Son of God was not the same person as Mary's son. According to him, these two persons were united first of all by inhabitation, in that the Word of God dwelt in the man Jesus as in a sanctuary; next, by unity of sentiments, in that the man's will was always conformable to that of the divine Person; finally, by unity of action, in so far as the man was the instrument made use of by the Word.

Nestorius was wrong concerning Christ because in his hypothesis, Jesus, however intimate his union with the Word, still remained a mere creature. Hence Mary would have been, not the true Mother of God, but the mother of a man who was united to the Son of God.

It would be wrong to suppose, however, that Nestorius and his followers made of Jesus nothing more than a mere man, entirely separable from the divine Word. This would certainly not have been the Jesus presented to us in the Gospels, who claimed to be God's Son in a unique manner, who had been conceived in Mary's womb by the power of God, so that he could be the Messiah, the Son of God.

If we keep in mind this union between Jesus and the Word of God, as Nestorius understood it, to illustrate the union between Mary the Immaculata and the Holy Spirit, we shall not be far from understanding Father Kolbe's way of looking at her as the spouse, the handmaid, and the living tabernacle of the Holy Spirit.

3. The Immaculata, Spouse of the Holy Spirit

On this point Father Kolbe follows the great tradition of the Fathers of the Church, which St. Louis Marie Grignion de Montfort made his own. Father Kolbe wrote to Father Vivoda:

The devotion taught by Blessed Grignion is ours exactly. (Letter, Dec. 4, 1933)

He further points out that the doctrinal basis for St. de Montfort's devotion lies in the fact that:

The Holy Spirit has made Mary his own spouse. (*Miles Immaculatae*, 1938, n. 2)

The image of the Holy Spirit and Mary as spouses shows that we have here two persons with two distinct wills, but that these two wills act as one.

The Mother of God is the most perfect of all creatures; she is immaculate, full of grace, all beautiful. From her God receives the highest glory a creature can possibly give him. So perfect is she, so closely bound to the Holy Spirit, that we can call her his spouse. (Conference, June 20, 1937)

Father Kolbe calls attention to the fact that this title of spouse of the Holy Spirit stresses the intimate union between the will of Mary and the unique will of the three divine Persons. This is precisely what he says in his testament-text of February 17, 1941:

In the union of the Holy Spirit with her, not only do we have the love of two beings; in one of the two we have all the love of the Trinity itself; and in the other we have all of creation's love. Hence, in this union heaven and earth meet; all of heaven with all of earth, the totality of divine eternal love with the plenitude of created love. It is the true summit of love. (Sketch, February 17, 1941)

Obviously, if Mary can be wed to the will of the Holy Trinity in the Holy Spirit, this is because she enjoys a very intimate union with him, so intimate that it transcends all that we can even imagine.

For Mary, as the spouse of the Holy Spirit and therefore raised above all created perfection, accomplishes in all things

45

the will of the Holy Spirit who dwells in her from the first instant of her conception. (*Miles Immaculatae*, 1938, n. 2)

4. The Immaculata, Handmaiden of the Holy Spirit

Father Kolbe has the flair of a true theologian; he possesses a fine feeling for analogies and illustrations. A single one is hardly sufficient to allow the feeble intellect of the believer to begin to grasp something of this mystery. This union between Mary Immaculate and the Holy Spirit, such as she affirms it in the apparitions at Lourdes, certainly implies that she is the one wedded to the will of God. Because of her closeness to the Holy Spirit in the Trinity, she desires nothing else but to love God, and everything that God loves, to such an extent that she identifies herself with the fruitful Power of the divine Love: "I am the Immaculate Conception." But the message of Lourdes does not contradict that of Nazareth. The one who speaks is still, as always, the handmaid of the Lord who knows so well how totally she lies in God's hands. This Father Kolbe realizes, too.

Into this world there comes the Immaculate one, with no slightest taint of sin, the masterpiece of God's hands, full of grace. God, in the Blessed Trinity, looks down on his handmaid's lowliness (i.e. her humility, the root of all virtues in her), and does great things in her, for he is the Almighty. (Notes, 1940)

The word "handmaid" suggests something different from the word "spouse." Husband and wife are two persons on a certain plane of equality, at least when united in love; each one keeps his own responsibility for the initiative of his actions, even though these tend to coalesce. A handmaid is one who abandons her own right to decide for herself; she allows herself to be commanded by a superior authority; she does this willingly, of course; still, her submission hands over to this superior authority the right to control her activity. The most apt image here is that of an instrument in the hands of an intelligent being, making use of it for his own purposes.

In all he does, God always wills to make use of instruments. . . . God, who gave us free will, wants us to serve him freely in the role of instruments, by bringing our wills into harmony with his, even as his Most Holy Mother did when she said: "Behold the handmaid of the Lord, let it be done to me according to thy word." (Conference, June 3, 1933)

Let us pray more and more that we may understand better and better what the Immaculata said at the moment of the Annunciation: "I am the handmaid of the Lord . . . let it be done as he wills." In this attitude alone will we find real happiness. This is the resumé of our mission on this earth. God made us to be his instruments . . . so, let us ask the Virgin Mary to teach us how our souls too can become the handmaids of the Lord. (Conference, April 2, 1938)

As a creature, as a *servant*, Mary embraces the will of the Lord on Annunciation Day. She is already with the Lord, and he with her; the angel says as much. It is up to the Lord to bring about within her whatever he wishes. One can sense how profoundly the Holy Spirit must already be living within her, as he comes to her anew in this moment when the Son of God is made flesh in her womb. In union with the Holy Spirit, who is God's Love personified, Mary pledges herself freely, from that moment on, to her role of divine motherhood.

Still, this comparison of the handmaid goes no further than to suggest a *moral* union, a union of *like sentiments* between the Trinity, in the Person of the Holy Spirit, and Mary. It does not completely clear up her use of the expression: "I am the Immaculate Conception."

The Holy Spirit dwells in the Immaculata, lives in her,

and does so from the first instant of her existence, and thenceforth forever. (Sketch, February 17, 1941)

5. The Immaculata, Sanctuary of the Holy Spirit

Mary's affirmation at Lourdes: "I am the Immaculate Conception" refers not only to her spiritual "I," but to the total, personal "I": to her body united to her soul as to its vital principle, both making up her personal reality.

It is in this perspective that we should consider the audacious words penned by Father Kolbe a few days prior to his arrest, and which constitute so to speak his last word on the subject:

Our heavenly Father is the source of all that is; everything comes from the Blessed Trinity. We cannot see God, and so Jesus came to this earth, to make him known to us. The Most Blessed Virgin is the one in whom we venerate the Holy Spirit, for she is his spouse.

Nothing very new so far; but then he goes on:

The third Person of the Blessed Trinity never took flesh; still, our human word "spouse" is far too weak to express the reality of the relationship between the Immaculata and the Holy Spirit. We can affirm that she is, in a certain sense the "incarnation" of the Holy Spirit. It is the Holy Spirit that we love in her; and through her we love the Son. The Holy Spirit is far too little known. . . . (Conference, February 5, 1941)

We recognize in these words Father Kolbe's great gifts as a theologian. He knows how to qualify what he states, thus permitting himself to say something which, without those qualifications, would not be theologically acceptable.[1] The divine mystery we are considering is truly ineffable; at times the human expressions we use seem contradictory. Thus, he says,

The Holy Spirit never took flesh;

and then declares,

> the Immaculata is, in a certain sense, the "incarnation" of the Holy Spirit.

In reality there is no contradiction here. Between Mary the Immaculata and the Holy Spirit there is a deep union not only because Mary's will is absolutely conformed with that of the Holy Spirit, as a dutiful spouse's would be, and also because she was always a conscious and free instrument in his regard, a true handmaid, but more precisely because the Holy Spirit dwells in her as in his privileged *sanctuary*.

The word *sanctuary* is the one the Council employs in speaking of the special relationship between Mary and the Holy Spirit:

> She benefitted by the Redemption in the most eminent manner, in consideration of the merits of her Son; and united with him by a close and indissoluble bond, she receives this tremendous responsibility and dignity of being the Mother of God's Son, and as a consequence, of being the Father's well-beloved daughter and the *sanctuary of the Holy Spirit*; this exceptional gift of grace places her far above all other creatures in Heaven and on earth. (*Lumen Gentium*, n. 53)

Sanctuary or temple: here we have a very concrete image. It indicates a material place totally reserved for God who resides there as Lord and Master. St. Paul does not hesitate to say: "Do you not know that your bodies are temples of the Holy Spirit who is in you, and whom you have received from God? Do you not know that you are not your own? For you have been bought at a great price! Glorify and bear God in your bodies" (1 Cor 6:19-20).

Mary herself depends on the Redemption wrought by Christ; it is a body exempt from sin by the foreseen merits of Christ, her Son and her Savior, that the Holy Spirit dwells as in his

49

sanctuary. This is what Father Kolbe means when he affirms that the Holy Spirit, who did not take flesh in Mary, yet lives in her, not only in her soul (as his spouse or handmaid) but in her body:

> The Immaculata is, in a certain sense, the "incarnation" of the Holy Spirit.

In a word, the Holy Spirit, without becoming incarnate in her, dwells in her totally, in her body and in her soul.

> It is said that the Holy Spirit dwells in the souls of the just. If this is so, then he must dwell in the most perfect manner possible in the soul of the Immaculata. Our Most Holy Mother is totally suffused with the divine. For this reason we call her the spouse of the Holy Spirit, even though we know that this name is only a distant shadow of the reality. For the Holy Spirit fashioned the humanity of Jesus in her womb, in a miraculous manner. If Jesus says of the souls of the just: "We will make our abode in them" (Jn 14: 23), then what an immense difference there must be between us and our most Blessed Mother, in regard to this indwelling! (Conference, April 9, 1938)

6. Immaculate, Because She Was to Be the Mother of God

To understand the very special mode of the Holy Spirit's indwelling in Mary, we must not lose sight of this profound and decisive truth:

> She was immaculate because she was to become the Mother of God; she became the Mother of God because she was immaculate. (Conference, July 26, 1939)

In this interconnection between the moment of Mary's conception in the womb of St. Anne, and the moment of Jesus' incarnation in Mary's womb, we find the key that unlocks the mystery of the deep union between Mary the Immaculata and the Holy Spirit.

Nobody can understand what a seed is, as a seed, so long as he has not seen it reach its perfect development by becoming a plant and producing its fruit. Only the fullgrown oak can reveal to us what an acorn really is.

To help his hearers understand the Kingdom of God, Jesus told them: "What shall we say the Kingdom of God is like, or with what shall we compare it? It is like a grain of mustard seed planted in the earth. This seed is smaller than all other seeds on earth. But once it has been planted, it grows up and becomes larger than all other herbs. It develops great branches so that the birds of the air can dwell under its shelter" (Mk 4:30-32).

In this passage we find both the means of recognizing the seed, and the idea that this seed, apparently the least of all, develops into the largest of garden herbs.

There is no better comparison to help us understand who Mary the Immaculata is. Her own conception in her mother's womb occurred without being noticed; no divine manifestation accompanied it then. We know nothing more about it than we do about other human conceptions. Moreover, she belonged to a very modest class of people; her parents lived unknown to most of their fellow citizens. So, when Mary's life began, nothing showed the world who she was. Mary herself says in the Magnificat: "He has bent down to the littleness of his handmaid" (Lk 1:48).

And yet she is predestined to become the Queen of Heaven and earth.

Humanly speaking, her case is difficult even to imagine. God does all sorts of marvelous things throughout the universe; he creates human beings who, since they possess intelligence, are capable of becoming his children in his kingdom, capable of becoming like him: "Look at the extraordinary charity the Father has endowed us with. Because of it we are called, and really are, the sons of God. Therefore . . . dearly beloved, we are now God's offspring, and it has not yet become clear what

51

we shall be. But we know that when he shall appear, we shall be like to him because we shall see him as he is" (1 Jn 3:1-2).

The grandiose destiny awaiting us even when we are only frail embryos in our mothers' wombs is almost unthinkable. But to no other creature, angelic or human, did God ever entrust his own Son, so that he could be brought forth into the world. Only the Virgin Mary was called to such a destiny.

She alone was created by God to become the Mother of God; for this she was fashioned by the Holy Spirit, so to speak, as a new creature. Her personal vocation was part and parcel of her nature as a woman; in body and in soul Mary exists only that she may be the Mother of God.

Whatever images we use, the reality is this. If we begin by accepting what revelation declares—that Mary is the Mother of God and that she was immaculate in her conception, so much so that she herself *is* the Immaculate Conception—we must admit that she was born of the Holy Spirit far more truly than she was born physically, carnally of her parents.

> It was necessary, *even before* the Virgin Mother of God was conceived by Anne, her mother, that grace should have been at work in her and produced its fruit; it was necessary that she who was to conceive the first-born of every creature should have herself been conceived as God's first-born daughter. (*Ineffabilis Deus,* Pope Pius IX)

This unique grace implies the *personal presence* of the Holy Spirit in her who was called to bring God's own Son into the world. Still, the Holy Spirit is not personally present in her as the Word is present in the flesh which he took in her womb. We repeat: the Word became flesh; the Holy Spirit did not become flesh. The personal presence of the Holy Spirit in Mary the Immaculata from the first instant of her life can be compared to the presence of the oak in the acorn, because all the specific nature of that oak is already contained in it, programmed into it, so to speak. The acorn is the oak in its germinal state, its state of living expectancy. But the entire nature of the oak is there already.

Because she was a woman, Mary, from the moment of her conception, possessed a nature adapted to human maternity, just as is the case with all other women, even in their mothers' wombs. What is special about Mary is that she was not called to be the human mother of a human son. Her special, unique vocation was to be the Mother of God; in other words, her maternity is inextricably bound up with the divine sonship of the One whom she will give birth to in the flesh. Her divine maternity, then, was already "programmed" as soon as she was conceived in the womb of Anne, her mother. Such a maternity undoubtedly implies the presence of the Holy Spirit.

We are not dealing here with the ordinary, natural presence by which God created her and preserved her being. Nor are we dealing with the special presence of God which makes every baptized person share, by grace, in God's own nature. Of course, Mary's soul, from the moment of her conception, was filled with sanctifying grace in a measure exceeding that given to any other creature which becomes God's child through baptism.

What we are concerned with here is a new sort of presence of the Holy Spirit, who unites her to himself in a manner proper and personal to himself, *as the divine source of all motherhood*. In other words, at the instant of Mary's conception, the Father and the Son joined this new creature to their common Spirit so that she might be capable of becoming the Mother of the Son through the Holy Spirit's action. From that moment on, in the depths of her being as a woman, this unique grace is operative and real, since by this grace the Immaculata is already defined, "programmed" if we dare say so, for her unique vocation, that of being the Mother of God.

Every man is born with the capacities required for the mission which God intends to entrust to him. (*Knight of the*

Immaculata, 1922, "The Grace of God and the Natural Gifts of the Saints")

Father Kolbe says it again, more precisely in his last text:
Among creatures made in God's image, the union brought about by married love is the most intimate of all. In a much more precise, more interior, more essential manner, the Holy Spirit lives in the soul of the Immaculata, in the depths of her very being. He makes her fruitful from the very first instant of her existence, all during her life, and for all eternity. This eternal "Immaculate Conception" (which is the Holy Spirit) produces, in an immaculate manner, divine life itself in the womb (or depths) of Mary's soul, making her the Immaculate Conception, the human Immaculate Conception. The virginal womb of Mary's body is kept sacred for him; there he conceives in time—because everything that is material happens in time—the human life of the man-God. (Sketch, February 17, 1941)

ENDNOTES

[1] Theologians prize accuracy in the formulation of truths to be believed because in them the human mind must find illumination, and correct order among the ideas these formulas evoke. Thus, one should avoid saying that "The Word became incarnate IN Jesus," but rather say "Jesus is the Incarnate Word of God." The former expression might lead one to think that the Word is IN the person of Jesus, as in a temple; that was more or less what Nestorius believed and taught.

On the other hand, one can certainly say, as Father Kolbe does, that "Mary Immaculate is, so to speak, the incarnation of the Holy Spirit." For while "the Holy Spirit did not take flesh" (and so Mary is not the Holy Spirit, as Jesus IS the Word), the Holy Spirit did come and dwell in Mary so intimately that she became his sanctuary, in her very being as a woman and as a mother. Hence the Holy Spirit did, so to speak, become incarnate IN Mary. But, to avoid all misunderstanding, it is preferable to say with Father Kolbe that "Mary is, so to speak, the incarnation of the Holy Spirit."

As Vatican II puts it, Mary is the temple, the sanctuary of the Holy Spirit. To understand better what this indwelling of the Holy Spirit in Mary means, think of a vase placed right in the heart of a bubbling spring. Not only does the vase fill with water; it overflows, so that those who come to drink can do so from the water contained in the vase, and drink all they want, so long as the vase remains in the spring. Mary, the Immaculata, united to the Holy Spirit, communicates to us this living water which refreshes all those who consecrate themselves to their Mother in the Spirit.

Chapter 4

THE HOLY SPIRIT'S MISSION IN THE IMMACULATA

W E NEED TO ASK OURSELVES THE FOLLOWING QUESTION, which has become so important today in this post-Conciliar period: "What is meant by a divine Person's *mission?*" It would be helpful to reread the documents of Vatican II, especially the Dogmatic Constitution *Lumen Gentium* as well as the Decree *Ad Gentes (On the Church's Mission Activity)*, where we are told that it is the Father, the First Principle of all, who sends his Son, and also the Holy Spirit to his Church, to make it truly a missionary Church.

What can we say about these personal missions confided to the Son and to the Holy Spirit? The answer to this question will enable us to glimpse in all its depth the mystery of the name Mary gave herself when she said "I am the Immaculate Conception."

It is Jesus Christ himself who speaks to us of his own mission and of the Holy Spirit's. Expressions such as, "The Father has sent me," and "I will send you the Holy Spirit," suggest under the form of images—for such was Jesus' customary manner of speaking to us of the mysteries of God and of his divine life—how the divine Persons came into our world. In the same vein he declares: "Your Father who is in Heaven." From on high the Father sends his Son to earth; and with the Son, who has "returned" to the bosom of his Father, he sends us the Holy Spirit. We must not, of course, allow these images to induce us to speak nonsense. "Our Father who art in Heaven" does not imply that the Father is far from us, or separated from Christ during his visible mission on this earth, because this would contradict the idea of an infinite and omnipresent God, and also the singleness of the divine nature in the Father, the Son, and the Holy Spirit. "He who sees me, sees my Father," said Jesus to St. Philip, because "I am in the Father, and the Father is in me" (Jn 14:9, 11). So then, the expression "The Father has sent me" does not mean that there can be any movement or change in God. God is immutable and eternal, one in three Persons. Jesus also said: "My Father and I are one." Neither should we imagine that the Holy Spirit, the personified Love proceeding from Father and Son, can ever actually *leave* the bosom of the Trinity.

In Father Kolbe s writings we find the usual language:

> Every action has the reaction in view. . . . God the Father is the First Principle and the last End. . . . action proceeds from the Father through the Son (as when Christ said: "I will send him to you"), and by the Holy Spirit (the Immaculata). The inverse reaction proceeds from the creature through the Immaculata (the Holy Spirit), and through Christ the Word, back to the Father. (Notes, 1939)

How then should we understand this expression: a "mission" of one of the divine Persons?

Here is a very simple comparison. A man on the earth's surface looks at the heavens and sees the sun apparently moving from east to west; but in fact the sun is motionless; it is the earth that turns. By this example, halting but expressive, we can say that "the Word was made flesh," although in reality it was not the Word that changed at all when he became flesh; on the contrary it was human nature that changed, that was taken up, that began to share divine life even while remaining a true human nature. A mission of a divine Person means a *new presence* of the Person who is sent, not a type of activity which would modify the essence of that divine Person. Sent to earth by his Father, Jesus always remains true God and true man; he is at the same time immortal and eternal, yet a member of our race, and one who after living on earth as a human being, subject to death as a result of Adam's sin, has achieved immortality.

The one whom the Father has sent into the world is his beloved Son, "in whom he is well pleased." Moved by the urging of their common love, the shared love of Father and Son, the Father sent his Son into the world. He gave his beloved Son to us. At the Son's baptism in the Jordan, the Father pointed out this gift of love he was giving to mankind when he sent the Spirit under the form of a dove to overshadow the head of Christ as he stepped from the waters. The Father wanted to show concretely that he had truly given us his Son: "God so loved the world that he gave it his only Son" (Jn 3:16). In the Spirit, who is the great Gift of God, the Primal Gift, the Son is thus *sent* and *given* to the world.

For we cannot separate the mission of the Son from that of the Holy Spirit, for the Father sends both of them in view of the same purpose: to bring back to himself all the creatures that had been scattered far from him by sin, yet which remained capable of being redeemed. "By the Holy Spirit (the Son) took flesh in the womb of the Virgin Mary" we say in the Creed. And when Christ *goes back* to the right hand of his Father, he continues his task, through the Spirit, until the end of the world.

We can see why, following Scripture, theologians insist in distinguishing, without separating, the missions of the Son and of the Holy Spirit. Jesus is the Incarnate Word, the Author of grace, the only Mediator between God and man. His personal mission took definite shape when he was conceived by a woman and became one of us, living a human life like ours in everything except sin. The Father sent his Son *not to the Virgin Mary*, but to the human creature formed within her by the Holy Spirit. As St. Paul puts it: "God sent his Son, *born* of a woman" (Gal 4:4). It is this perspective that opens the chapter on the Virgin Mary in the Dogmatic Constitution *Lumen Gentium* (chapter 8).

Again, it is to the Virgin herself that the Holy Spirit is sent and given: "For it was by the descent of the Holy Spirit on the Virgin Mary that Christ was conceived" says the Council (*Ad Gentes*, n. 4). Let us recall here the saying of Father Kolbe:

> She was immaculate because she was to become the Mother of God; she became the Mother of God because she was immaculate.

Whereas the union between the human and the divine was immediately perfect in Christ, the Incarnate Word, the union between the Most Blessed Virgin and the Holy Spirit grew progressively closer. It was already a reality the moment this privileged creature came into being; it consecrated her, in the Annunciation, as the Mother of God. This union became perfect in the person of the Immaculata when she was assumed into the glory of Heaven. From that moment on, Mary is truly the woman clothed with the sun; and this union will achieve its total completeness when, together with all the elect, Mary will form the Heavenly Jerusalem, and accompany Christ in his final glory.

As we know, the mission of a divine Person requires three conditions: 1) there must be a new sort of presence of the Person who is sent, in the creature(s) to whom he is sent; 2) the sending of the divine Person corresponds with the order of origin in the Trinity itself: The Father alone sends the Son; the Father and the Son together send the Holy Spirit; 3) the creature who receives this mission has been created especially for this purpose.

1) As Father Kolbe repeats so often, the Holy Spirit is not present in the Virgin Mary in the same way in which the Word is present in the humanity of Christ which was conceived in Mary's womb. But in both cases we have a *new* mode of presence of the Son and of the Holy Spirit. We say that the Son has really been sent, because there is a real presence of this second Person in the human nature which he assumed. Jesus is the true Son of the Father. The change is not in the Person who is sent—eternal and immutable as he is—but in the humanity which is united to the Word in his very essence of Sonship to the Father.

In the same way we should say that the Holy Spirit is really sent to Mary, because she is his privileged dwelling place and sanctuary. The same Spirit who from all eternity is the Immaculate Conception in the bosom of the Trinity, makes of Mary another Immaculate Conception. The change is not in the Person who has been sent, for he too is eternal and immutable, but in this creature who was, from her life's first moment, united to the third Person, the source of all fruitful Love, the primary Gift and divine mother-like fruitfulness of Love.

Reread the words of Father Kolbe in his last writing:

> This eternal Immaculate Conception (which is the Holy Spirit) produces, in an immaculate manner, divine life itself in the womb (or depths) of Mary's soul, making her the Immaculate Conception, the human Immaculate Conception. The virginal womb of Mary's body is kept sacred for him: there he conceives in time—because everything that is material happens in time—the human life of the Man-God. (Sketch, February 17, 1941)

He had written, in formula style, in Latin:

> Filius incarnatus est: Jesus Christus.
> Spiritus Sanctus quasi incarnatus est: Immaculata.
> (The Son is incarnate: Jesus Christ. The Holy Spirit is quasi incarnate: the Immaculata.)

Bold words indeed! But, faced with the words Mary spoke at Lourdes: "I AM the Immaculate Conception," there is really nothing else to say, unless we wish to suppose that Mary was then giving herself only a symbolic name. Moreover, these bold words are those of an expert theologian; he uses the necessary restriction, "*quasi incarnatus*," which forces the mind of the believer to open itself up to the mystery, while not disturbing its faith. He constantly maintains that the Son alone was truly made man, not the Holy Spirit.

The task of the theologian is not to demonstrate the ineffable, but to try to express it if he can in terms which will provoke the heart of the believer to go beyond what the mind can understand. The Holy Spirit is "*quasi*" (*in some manner*) incarnate, without being really and strictly incarnate; for Mary the Immaculata is, as such, taken up by the Holy Spirit in all her being, as a woman and as a mother.

2) This leads us to define more precisely the second condition needed for a true mission by a divine Person.

It is the Father alone who sends the Son, who gives him to this humanity that he assumes into union with his own Person.

The Holy Spirit is sent by both Father and Son to the Virgin, given to her by them, so that she may conceive this humanity which the Word will take unto himself. The coming of the Spirit pre-exists, in time, the coming of the Son, precisely because the Son sends the Spirit, in the Father's name, to a daughter of Adam at the very instant when she was conceived. In other words, it was the Holy Spirit who came to Mary from the Father by the Son, to make of her the Immaculate Conception, the Gift of Love, the future Mother of God, just as he himself draws his origin from the Father through the Son in the bosom of the Trinity, where he is from all eternity their mutual Love, their primary Gift to each other, the divine motherhood of love.

3) Finally, in the external missions of the Son and of the Holy Spirit there is another specific condition which authenticates this mission; it always takes place in a being *created on purpose* for this at that very moment. The Son entered the human body and soul which had been created at that very instant of his Incarnation. So too, in every external mission of the Holy Spirit, theologians tell us, following the Scriptures, we find "a creature" specially brought into being for the purpose of signifying his presence: the dove hovering over the head of Jesus at his baptism, the tongues of fire and the wind on Pentecost.

In the case of the Most Blessed Virgin there was not only signifying, but complete possessing. Indeed, at the moment of the Incarnation the sign is joined immediately to the reality which it manifests: a Virgin conceives a child by the overshadowing Power of the Holy Spirit. "The Holy Spirit shall come upon thee, and the power of the Most High will overshadow thee; thus the Holy One who will be born of thee shall be called the Son of God" (Lk1:35). Here is the sign promised by God and announced by the prophet Isaiah: "The Lord himself will give you a sign: behold the virgin shall conceive and bring forth a son" (Is 7:14).

It is even truer to say of Mary than of the other symbols of the Holy Spirit's presence—the dove, the tongues of fire— that this mother was *created on purpose* to show by her virginal motherhood the presence of the Holy Spirit in her. Every other woman finds in her motherhood the *raison d'etre* of her existence, naturally and supernaturally, so that as St. Paul says, "she shall be saved by child-bearing" (1 Tm 2:15). But of course no woman is created exclusively *to be* a mother and nothing else; her destiny is first of all individual, personal. Otherwise we would be forced to conclude that no woman who has not known motherhood could ever reach her perfection before God. On the contrary, Mary was created solely to be a mother, the mother of God. Such is her eternal destiny. She exists only to be a mother. This is something which enriches beyond all counting her own personal life. From all eternity God foresaw her and willed that she should exist, so that she might receive in time the mission of the Holy Spirit, who comes "to renew the face of the earth."

Between her and the other symbolic realities created to give notice of the presence of the Holy Spirit, there is this further difference: Mary was created not only as a sign of the Holy Spirit's presence, but as a unique sanctuary, a living, willing collaboratrix with him, in love, as his handmaid and spouse. She partakes of this divine presence in giving up not only all she has, but all she is, to the Spirit by whom Christ was conceived in her womb. The Virgin is an intelligent creature; hence she can personally possess the Spirit who comes to fulfill in her his own divine mission of motherhood in love toward the Son sent in the flesh to save all men.

In the two pivotal events of Mary's life—her creation by God and her acceptance of his call to be the Mother of his Son—we recognize the two moments of "action" and "reaction" (or of "separation" and "union"), the well known images of Father Kolbe.

Here again is what he wrote in his testament-text:

First, God creates the universe; that is something like a separation; then creatures, by following the natural law given to them by God, reach their perfection, become like him, and go back to him. Intelligent creatures love him in a conscious manner; through this love they unite themselves more and more closely with him, and so find their way back to him. The creature most completely filled with this love, filled with God himself, was the Immaculata, who never contracted the slightest stain of sin, who never departed in the least from God's will. United to the Holy Spirit as his spouse, she is one with God in an incomparably more perfect way that can be predicated of any other creature. (Sketch, February 17, 1941)

Mary was created to be, for eternity, the Mother of God's Son. In giving God her full and unqualified assent, Mary "reacted" to the "action" of God. She united herself to the One who had created her. She went back to the Father through the Son, in an inseparable union with the Spirit who had come to her from the moment of her Immaculate Conception.

We can understand how fitting it was that Mary the Immaculata should have told Bernadette: "I am the Immaculate Conception" on the 25th of March, the day on which the Church celebrates the Incarnation. The same Spirit who shaped the body of Christ in his mother, shaped the body of Mary herself. The *fruit* of the Virgin's womb indicates the nature of the *fruit* of Anne's womb. Jesus, the stainless One, yet a man, the first-born of every creature, was like every child born of woman, conceived in the likeness of the one who bore him, namely Mary, the Immaculata, the Woman, the first-born daughter of every creature. Without doubt Jesus depends on Mary his mother only for his human nature; the Immaculata was, on the contrary, created to be in the Holy Spirit entirely conformable to the Son of God, the divine Word whom she now beholds and loves in her glorious state as Mother of God and Immaculate Conception.

If in this union between Mary and the Holy Spirit there always remain two distinct persons—this creature, and the third Person of the Blessed Trinity—they still share a single motherhood: the divine Maternity of love which unites the Son to the Father.

> And so the return to God, that is to say, the equal but contrary reaction (which is love) follows a different path from that found in creation. . . . This return trail goes from the Spirit through the Son back to the Father; in other words, by the Spirit the Son becomes incarnate in the womb of the Immaculata, and through the Son love returns to the Father. . . . If among human beings the wife

takes the name of her husband because she belongs to him, is one with him, becomes equal to him, and is with him the source of new life, with how much greater reason should not the name of the Holy Spirit, who is the divine Immaculate Conception, be used as the name of her in whom he lives as uncreated Love, the principle of life in the whole supernatural order of grace? (Sketch, February 17, 1941)

Chapter 5

THE IMMACULATA, SUMMIT OF CREATION

Every creature, and everything in creation, comes into existence through God's action. God alone exists of himself. Everything else receives its being, moment by moment, from God; this is true even of Jesus' humanity. Our Lady also is a creature made by God. In this sense, and of herself, she is nothing. Everything she possesses was given to her by God. (Conference, April 9, 1938)

IT IS PROPER TO REMIND OURSELVES THAT THE VIRGIN MARY IS a creature, a human person, whereas the humanity of Christ does not constitute a human person. This is why the man Jesus is the true Son of God, unique because he is both divine and human. Mary is not the Holy Spirit in person, but she lives fully the life of the Spirit.

The Holy Spirit is the great Gift of God. Before a gift is bestowed it belongs entirely to the donor, once it has been conferred it belongs to the donee. Before he was "given," the Holy Spirit was the pure relationship between the Father and the Son from whom he draws his being eternally. But from the moment of the Virgin's conception in the womb of her mother St. Anne, the Holy Spirit was *given* to this new creature. Between the Most Blessed Virgin and the Holy Spirit there was set up a relationship which, without introducing any change in the immutable Gift of God, made of this human creature the gift of God *outside of God.* St. Louis de Montfort had grasped this very well when he called the Virgin Mother of God "our link with God." The Holy Spirit occupies with such overwhelming power the personal being of Mary the Immaculata, that she was from the moment she was created a "pure link with God."

All other spiritual creatures depend on their Creator in the natural possession of their being by themselves—this is true of every spiritual being, angelic or human. Mary the Immaculata on the contrary, does not possess herself by herself; she possesses herself by the Holy Spirit.

For the Holy Spirit is *her* spirit. Far from being alienated in her personality because of the dominance of the Holy Spirit, she is on the contrary more than any other creature in full possession of herself. It is characteristic of God that he acts in us in such a manner that our actions are truly ours. Of herself, Mary the Immaculata is not God; she possesses existence apart from God, unlike Christ who is God himself, the Son of the Father. But she lives only in a state of divine synergy with the Holy Spirit, "the Lord and giver of life."

> True, the Immaculata is made by God, and like any other work of God she is incomparably inferior to him because she depends on him completely. But she is the holiest, most perfect of creatures. According to St. Bonaventure, "God could have created a greater and more perfect world than this one; but even he could not have made anything higher in dignity than Mary. (*Knight of the Immaculata,* 1938)

And to bring out the fact that the greatness of this creature shows itself not only in God's action upon her, but also in her *reaction* as a creature, in her *returning* to God, he does not hesitate to say:

The summit of love on the part of creatures who turn back to God, is the Immaculata: the creature that knew no spot of sin, that is all beautiful, all divine. Her will never turned aside in the slightest from God's will. With all the energy of her will she attached herself to God. (Sketch, 1940)

Jesus is not merely divine; he is God, God the Son. Mary is not God, but she is fully divine because, as a creature, she has no life except in her relationship with God: with the Father whose daughter she is; with the Son, whose mother she is; with the Holy Spirit, whose unique sanctuary she is.

Spiritual beings are created in God's image and likeness. Of Mary we can say that she is God's daughter. (Conference, April 9, 1938)

As a creature she is close to us; as God's own Mother she approaches divinity. (Conference, July 3, 1938)

When we honor the Immaculata we are, very specifically, adoring the Holy Spirit. (Letter to Fr. Salezy Mikolajczyk, July 28, 1938)

This helps us understand better Mary's affirmation at Lourdes: "I am the Immaculate Conception," even though it remains a divine, insoluble mystery.

In a passage written in Latin, in which he was seeking to throw some light on the mystery of Mary's being, Father Kolbe once more underscores this affirmation.

Mother of God! . . . Here our feeble intellect fails us in our effort to grasp the infinite dignity of God, and consequently, the greatness of the Mother of God. God is Love. Out of the overflowing abundance of his own life the Father begets the Son, and the Spirit proceeds from Father and Son. . . . From all eternity God had foreseen this creature who, in absolutely no way however slight would ever deviate from his will, who would lose no grace, who would never attribute to herself what he would give her. The Giver of grace, the Holy Spirit, dwelt in her soul from the very first instant of her existence; he penetrated her being to such depths that to call her the spouse of the Holy Spirit is to use a pale, distant, most inadequate (even though correct) comparison to express their union. He did not allow her to be stained by Original Sin; and so she was conceived without sin, conceived immaculate.

At Lourdes the Immaculate Virgin replied to St. Bernadette who asked her who she was, by saying: "I am the Immaculate Conception." By these luminous words she tells us not only that she was immaculate in her conception, but beyond this that she is the Immaculate Conception as such. Something white is one thing; the whiteness of a thing is something else. Something perfect is one thing; the perfection of a thing is something else. When God said to Moses "I am the One who is," God was telling him: "What is proper to my essence is that I should always be, by my very nature, of myself, with no other principle of being." The immaculate Virgin of course, was created by God; she is a creature; she is a conception; still, she is the Immaculate Conception! What depths of mystery lie hidden in those words!

And just as everything in the natural and in the supernatural orders comes down from the Father through the Son and the Spirit upon creatures, so, in like manner, all creatures go back to the Father by the Spirit and by the Son.

But the Immaculate Virgin, the most perfect of all creatures, has been raised above all others, and shares in the divinity in an unspeakable manner.[1]

This passage, which repeats the themes dear to Father Kolbe, goes farther in striving to express what the nature of this ineffable creature really is like. Understandably, he keeps coming back to Lourdes. Mary, in telling Bernadette her name, wishes first of all to confirm the dogma of her Immaculate Conception, defined four years earlier. She did not answer Bernadette until March 25, because:

If she was immaculate, it was so that she might be the Mother of God.

The feast of the Annunciation, as we have previously mentioned, pointed this up very appositely. Finally, she who appeared to St. Bernadette was already enjoying the glory of her Assumption and her crowning as Queen of Heaven. What was, at the start of her life, only like a seed, had come to full flowering in the bosom of the Trinity where she definitively dwells. She no longer has a physical, material body; her body is glorified; and it is this whole being of hers in glory that is her true "I," her real self, her "hypostasis" one might say. No doubt, she always remains a true creature; yet more than ever the "I am" pronounced by this woman is assimilated to, without ever being confounded with, the Holy Spirit, the Immaculate Conception of the Love of the Father and the Son. Through the Holy Spirit, Mary is also assimilated to the Word, who is the Conception of the Father's thought. In this way she is totally given by the Son to the Father, as his well-beloved daughter. So then, when the Most Blessed Virgin told Bernadette: "I am the Immaculate Conception," she was referring to the double conception of thought and of love that exists in the bosom of the Trinity. Can our language go any farther while remaining true to the faith we profess? Hardly. The Most Blessed Virgin said all that can be said; she has revealed to us that she and the Holy Spirit together make up a single maternity of love with regard to the Father's Son, in God who is love.

Someone might perhaps object that this revelation concerning Mary took place at Lourdes; hence it is not the infallible voice of the Church officially teaching revealed truth. This

71

objection, however, is without solid foundation; for the Most Blessed Virgin did not say anything more of herself than Pope Pius IX had recently declared in his Bull *Ineffabilis Deus* (1854). True, the precise language used by Mary at Lourdes in 1858 is not to be found explicitly in the Bull. But the Pope did show that the physical conception of Mary in the womb of her mother took second place with regard to her eternal, divine election, by which she became Gods first-born daughter in order to bring forth his first-born Son. In doing this, Pius IX invited the faithful to consider Mary as having been raised immediately to a rank surpassing that of every other creature. Moreover, after all that has taken place at Lourdes, after millions of Christians have accepted as being conformable to their understanding of the faith those words inscribed around the statue in the grotto of Massabielle, who would dare to say that we do not find here an application of the well known principle "*vox populi, vox Dei*," or of this other maxim, "*lex orandi, lex credendi*"?

Here is what Father Kolbe himself remarked:

> The miracle of the Resurrection is the basis of our faith. Jesus' disciples were weak even though they had seen many miracles; when he was arrested all of them abandoned him. Only after Jesus had risen again was their faith strengthened; only afterwards did they find the courage to endure suffering and persecution.
>
> Since Jesus' Resurrection, from time to time miracles occur to strengthen our faith, such as those which happen at Lourdes. There the Immaculata chose a frail instrument to show her power all the more clearly. At the time there were many objections; people said "it isn't true." But all the while the miraculous water was flowing, and many miracles and conversions took place. Well then, what did the Most Blessed Virgin do amidst all these marvelous occurrences? In the presence of all these people she declared who she was, thus confirming the dogma of the

Immaculate Conception defined in 1854. She said: "I am the Immaculate Conception." If she is the Immaculate Conception, then whatever serves as the groundwork of this truth is also true. Thus this apparition at Lourdes is a confirmation of the whole Catholic faith. This is why these apparitions have such profound importance. (Conference, February 11, 1938)

Speaking of Mary, once her amazing, ineffable declaration at Lourdes had become known, the liturgy of the Church invites us to ponder her mystery in the light of God's word. The following passage, ordinarily so difficult to explain, takes on a real, not merely symbolic, meaning if we think of it as pronounced by the Immaculata herself, intimately united as she was with the Holy Spirit, the divine Inspirer of this text:

> The Lord begot me in the beginning before he planned anything, before the most ancient of his works; from eternity I was established, before anything began, before the earth. Before the abysses were created I was already conceived . . . I was with him then, arranging everything. And day after day I found delight playing before him all the while, playing on the surface of the earth; and my delight was to be with the sons of men. (Prv 8:22-24, 30-31)

If Mary, as a humble daughter of Adam, came into existence only after innumerable generations of human beings, she was already present in God's own mind, outside of all time, in the Holy Spirit himself. In God's eternal NOW, where she exists forever, she lives and reigns as the sovereign Mother, above all other creatures, cooperating in God's divine task of governing the world, embracing the entire scope of creation, before her and after her.

This is why Father Kolbe does not hesitate to identify Mary with Wisdom, "the artificer of all" (Wis 7:22).

73

She is, [he says, applying to her the words of the Sacred Author] a breath of divine power, a most pure effusion of the Most High; hence nothing sullied can ever contaminate her. She is a reflection of the eternal light, a spotless mirror of God's activity, an image of his excellence. . . . She is indeed more beautiful than the sun, surpasses all the constellations, and compared to light itself, she is more brilliant. (Wis 7:25-26, 29, as in Sketch, 1940)

We must acknowledge, [he goes on] that in his creative omnipotence God made the Immaculata all holy. As a creature she is close to us; as Mother of God she touches divinity itself. The Immaculata is the summit of perfection, of holiness achievable by creatures. No one else could ever attain this degree of grace; only the Mother of God could ever reach it. (Conference, July 3, 1938)

Twenty-five years later, the Second Vatican Council would say this very same thing, echoing Paul VI: "She occupies in the Holy Church the highest rank after Christ himself, and at the same time she is the closest to us" (*Lumen Gentium*, n. 54).

If we refer to Mary the Immaculata the double conception of thought and of love found in God—the Word and the Holy Spirit—we may say that the Father, in a way infinitely better than that of the most gifted artist, makes Mary the exemplar and matrix of the visible and invisible universe which he has conceived as an ideal in his mind before attempting to translate it into material reality. Thus in her he sees before him a model that represents his ideal in mock-up. On each occasion the artist must reshape his model in order to express a different work, conceived along other lines; but the Father, through his one Word full of Love, sees in the Immaculata the entire universe in all its rich multiplicity and harmonious unity.

Now we can understand better why Father Kolbe goes so far as to say:

The Immaculate Conception belongs to the Virgin's very essence . . . this name she used at Lourdes is fully justified in all of her life, because she is always immaculate, hence "full of grace"; because "God is always with her," even to that astounding degree of intimacy that makes her Mother of his Son. (Sketch, 1940)

Because of this she holds the first place in the history of salvation. Oriental Christianity understood this very well when it gave her the name "*Panagia*" (all holy), the same name it gives to the Holy Spirit himself: "*Panagion*."

Endnotes

[1] In *Miles Immaculatae*, I, 1938, p. 294, Father Kolbe goes so far as to say in a note written in 1939 that with the affirmation of our Lady at Lourdes, one could say that Mary is "Immaculation." He invented this neologism in Polish. We reproduce it here literally.

Chapter 6

The Immaculata
and the Church

1. God's Plan of Salvation

IN AN ILLUMINATING PASSAGE, FATHER KOLBE SKETCHED GOD'S plan of salvation:

Among the innumerable possible beings that could express his different perfections, God from all eternity saw one endowed with perfect form, immaculate, with no slightest taint of sin, a creature that would reflect his own divine qualities in the most perfect degree possible for a created nature. He rejoiced in this vision, and from all eternity decided that in due time he would call such a creature into existence.

When he had created the angels, God willed that they should spontaneously give him a proof that they should always and everywhere accomplish his will. He revealed to them the mystery of the Incarnation: that some day he would call into existence a human creature made of body and soul, a creature that he would raise to the dignity of Mother of God; consequently she would be their Queen whom they must venerate. A great multitude of these angelic spirits hailed with joy this woman whom their Creator had determined to elevate to so sublime a degree of dignity, and in all humility they paid homage to their future Sovereign. But some of them, led by Lucifer, insolently forgetting that whatever they were and had, had been bestowed on them by God, and that of themselves they were absolutely nothing, revolted against God's will to which they refused to submit. They considered themselves far superior to every human being made of flesh and blood. To pay homage to a woman seemed to them a derogation to their dignity; they fell into pride and refused to go along with God's will.

Beeause of this they were punished immediately, eternally. They were banished from God's presence and hurled into hell. Being pure spirits, they possessed keen intellects; for this reason their action had been fully conscious and willful. Their crime had all the characteristics of a mortal sin, since they fully consented to what they did. Hence, from being angels they became demons forever. From that moment onward the demons have never forgotten that vision of the Immaculata, who became for the good angels the occasion of their being confirmed in grace and the pledge of their eternal happiness, while on the other hand she had proved the stumbling block fatal to the wicked angels, and the occasion of their being rejected by God. Because of this the demons' anger flared up against her, an infernal hatred just like that which they entertain toward God himself, whose faithful image she is.

In the earthly paradise, Satan saw a being that resembled the woman he hated. Realizing that he could never do anything to God or to Mary herself, he resolved to direct his malevolence against the ancestress of Mary, against the first mother of all humanity, Eve. He suceeded in making her reject God's will, and in having her try to find her perfection not in yielding to God's designs but in acting in accord with her own reason. She too was overcome by pride.

Man who knows things through his senses is far indeed from the clear knowledge possessed by purely spiritual beings; for this reason his sins are far less grievous. . . . It was then that God in his mercy promised humanity a Redeemer, while he predicted to the devil that his conquest of Eve, the mother of the future woman who had been foretold, would not change his divine plan. She would still "crush his head," even though Satan would "lie in wait for her heel without respite." (Sketch, 1940)

2. The Woman Clothed With the Sun; the New Jerusalem

Paul VI in his beatification homily did not hesitate to say that Father Kolbe:

made of the devotion to the mother of God, whom he contemplated clothed in the splendor of the sun, the focal point of his spirituality, of his apostolate, of his theology. . . . Kolbe, with the whole of Catholic liturgy and spirituality, sees Mary as part of the divine plan, as the "unvarying aim of God's eternal design," as the being full of grace, as the seat of wisdom, as the one predestined to be the Mother of Christ, as the queen of the messianic kingdom, and yet as the humble handmaid of the Lord, the one chosen to offer her irreplaceable cooperation in the Incarnation of the Word, the mother of the Man-God, our Savior. Mary is the one thanks to whom Jesus comes to mankind. (October 17, 1971)

Father Kolbe does indeed see in the Immaculate Lady of Lourdes the one who is henceforth in Heaven, body and soul, and who reigns over the kingdom of her Son. At Lourdes the crowned statue of the Virgin in the esplanade is the object of tender devotion; it is constantly surrounded with flowers; and innumerable pilgrims gather there to pray in silence.

"A great sign appeared in the heavens: a woman clothed with the sun, with the moon under her feet, and on her

79

head a crown of twelve stars. She was with child, and she wailed aloud in pain as she labored to give birth" (Rev 12:1-2). After the struggle between Michael and his angels against "the dragon, who is the devil and Satan," and after Michael's victory, 'a voice rang out in the heavens: 'Now have salvation and power come, the reign of our God, and the authority of his anointed One; for the accuser of our brothers is cast out, who night and day accused them before God. . . .'" (Rev 10-11; Sketch, 1940)

This first victory is the Resurrection of Christ and the glory of the first martyrs; the woman could not be reached by the dragon, who "went to persecute the rest of her children." Finally there will come about the definitive victory of the Woman when she appears in all her glory with all her children, like a new city, the heavenly Jerusalem:

Then I saw a new heaven and a new earth. The first heaven and the first earth had passed away, and there was then no sea. I, John, saw the the holy city, the new Jerusalem, coming down out of heaven from God, as a bride prepared to meet her husband. I heard a powerful voice from the throne say: "This is God's dwelling among men. He shall dwell with them and they shall be his people, and he shall be their God who is always with them. He shall wipe away every tear from their eyes, and there shall be no more death or mourning, crying out, or pain, for the first things have passed away." The One who sat on the throne said to me: "See, I make all things new." (Rev 21:1-5)

We are living between these two points in time, so to speak: between the Pentecost-Church on the one hand, which was born of Christ's Resurrection, of his personal victory over Satan; and on the other, the Church of the last days at the end of the world, full of light and glory, the new Jerusalem. Father Domanski is right in saying that:

80

Father Kolbe fixes his gaze on the Immaculata and sees her as the Church presents her to us in the book of Genesis and in Christian art, in particular as she appears on the Miraculous Medal and in the liturgical texts, where she is called "all beautiful, spotless, formidable as an army drawn up for battle" (Song 6:4). (*Miles Immaculatae*, n. 4, 1973; Sketch, 1940)

The apparitions of our Lady at the Rue du Bac in 1830, which along with those of Lourdes Father Kolbe always held in deep veneration, teach us that Mary is all powerful in the Church's struggle against evil. Her strength derives from the victory won by her Son, thanks to which she herself was protected from all sin and preserved immaculate. Father Kolbe felt inspired to take his place too in this "army drawn up for battle," and to enroll as many Christians as possible along with him. Together with a few friends, he founded the Militia of the Immaculata in Rome on October 16, 1917, hoping to make it an army of true spiritual warriors who would consecrate themselves to Mary the Immaculata in order to hasten the coming of the kingdom of Christ her Son.

Three days previously, on October 13, 1917, the most Blessed Virgin had appeared at Fatima resembling John's vision of the Heavenly Jerusalem. It does not seem that Father Kolbe ever heard of the apparitions at Fatima; before the war they had scarcely been spoken of outside of Portugal. But the year after he died Pope Pius XII, on October 31, 1942, consecrated the entire world to the Immaculate Heart of Mary, in partial response to one of the wishes expressed by the glorious Virgin of Fatima. Above the altar dedicated to St. Maximilian Kolbe at Niepokalanow there is a painting that shows Pius XII making this act of consecration.

The Apocalypse contains the most eloquent testimonial to the bond between our Lady and the Church, [declares Father A. Feuillet]. What John beheld is like an ikon repre-

81

senting the Church at the end of the world under the form of this woman clothed with the sun, already victorious over the infernal dragon, even before she gives birth, amid dreadful agony, to the Messiah and his people on earth. Just as the stars (angels) of the seven letters in the Apocalypse almost certainly stand for the leaders of the various Christian communities (St. Polycrates of Ephesus called the apostles and the first great monarchical bishops of Asia alike "great stars": *Eusebius, HE XXIV,* 2-6), we can plausibly believe that the twelve stars in the crown worn by the Woman of the Apocalypse refer to the twelve Apostles who founded the Church.

The entire history of the salvation of men, sinful children of Adam, contains but one name that escapes this universal deluge of sin: one human creature of Adam's race: Mary. Not that she is outside of the influence of the Redeemer, for, as Father Kolbe says:

> God told the demon that his victory over Eve, the mother of the woman whom he had promised (Mary), would not change the divine plans.

This is why we must always think of this unique creature in terms of the destruction of sin, and of death, the wages of sin.

Because of this, although she came into the world preceded by thousands of generations of men and women, Mary, in God's eternal plan which is immutable, stands at the very summit of the whole creation, exalted over all other creatures angelic or human, the first-born daughter who is next to the first-born Son. Indeed, the parable of the mustard seed, planted in the earth and which becomes the greatest of garden herbs, finds here a marvelous application, beyond all imagining or reasoning.

The Virgin could be shown to the angels as soon as they themselves had been created, as their queen and sovereign, even though she herself did not exist as yet materially in the body. So at least opines Father Kolbe. Since Mary is the Immaculate Conception among creatures, she was manifested to the angels as being united to the Holy Spirit in person, as the Mother and Queen of all creatures.

3. The Immaculata Is the Church 'Par Excellence'

Inseparable as she is from the Holy Spirit, Mary the Immaculata is the Church *par excellence*.

Mary was already the Church—even more truly than the seed is, substantially, already the plant—when she was fashioned by the Holy Spirit as the Immaculate Conception at the very start of her existence.

Mary is already the Church when, at the Annunciation, she conceives Jesus, the Head of the Mystical Body, through the power of the Holy Spirit, beneath whose shadow she "gives her active and free consent to this event that will be decisive for all future ages" (Paul VI, *Marialis Cultus*, February 2, 1974).

Mary is already the Church when, as the Mother of Sorrows at the foot of the cross "standing there in accordance with a divine design" (*Lumen Gentium*, n. 58), she brings forth in sorrow the mystical body "which Christ loved, and for which he gave himself up, so as to purify it, cleansing it by the laver of water in the word of life; that he might present it to himself a glorious Church not having spot or wrinkle or any such thing, but that it should be holy and without blemish" (Eph 5:25-27). On Calvary, Mary completed in her own body what was still wanting for her in the sufferings of Christ (cf. Col 1:24), and so became the associate of Christ the Redeemer, the Co-Redemptrix. From that time on she can truly be called the "Mother of the Living," the new Eve; and to signify this Jesus gave her to John as a mother at the very moment when he was about to expire (Jn 19:27; cf. v. 26).

Mary is already the Church on Pentecost, when, after having

prayed along with the Apostles, "calling down by her prayers also the gift of the Spirit who, in the Annunciation had already overshadowed her" (*Lumen Gentium*, n. 59), she became "the Mother of the Shepherds and of the faithful, in a word, Mother of the entire Church" (Paul VI, November 21, 1964). Almost a quarter of a century before this pronouncement made during Vatican II, Father Kolbe had said:

> Whoever does not wish to have Mary Immaculate as his Mother will not have Christ as his Brother either; the Father will not send his Son to him; the Son will not descend into his soul; the Holy Spirit will not make him a member of the mystical body of Christ; for all these mysteries of grace take place in Mary full of grace, and in her alone. No other creature is or will ever be immaculate like her, or full of grace, or capable of being so intimately united to the Lord as was the Immaculate Virgin. And since the first-born Son, the Man-God, was conceived only through the specific consent of the Most Blessed Virgin, the same holds true of all other humans, who must imitate in all things their primary model, Christ. (Sketch, 1940)

Mary will be the Church in all its fullness when, on the last day she appears in all her glory as the new Jerusalem, together with all the elect, at the moment when the King of glory, "the seed of David, the bright morning star," will reply to the last supplication of the "Spirit and the Bride" who call to him incessantly, "Come!" (cf. Rev 22:16-17).

In this way Mary the Immaculata, through the divine power of the Love of the Father and the Son, is the mistress of the whole history of salvation.

> Till the end of time Satan will never give up tempting men, setting up obstacles to their salvation, and combatting them; but he will do all this only within the limits allowed him by the Immaculata; this means, only in so far as this is

necessary to enable us to reap the merits of our victory, which will be certain if we fight the battle under her standard, with her, through her, by her and in her. (Letter to Fr. Florian Koziura, March 2, 1931)

There is much evil in the world, but let us not forget that the Immaculata is more powerful yet, and that she will "crush the infernal serpent's head." (Letter to a reader of *Knight of the Immaculata*, September 12, 1924)

As he wrote to his mother, the triumph of Mary is the triumph of the Holy Spirit; and this triumph is already obvious even in our times:

Our era is the era of the Immaculata, or, as others put it, the era of the Holy Spirit. The infernal serpent shows his head all over the world; but Mary will crush him and win decisive victories, even though he constantly seeks to bite her heel. (March 15, 1936)

Paul VI calls attention in his beatification homily to "the characteristic although by no means original aspect of Blessed Kolbe's devotion—his 'hyperdulia'—towards the most Blessed Virgin." It is:

the importance which, faced with the needs of the Church today, he attributes to the effectiveness of her prophecy concerning the glory of the Lord and the exaltation of the humble, to the power of her intercession, to the marvelous examples she has given us, and to the presence of her motherly love for us. The Council has confirmed us in our certainty about these things; and today, from Heaven, Father Kolbe teaches us how to take them to heart and to live by them.

As Mother of the Church, Mary the Immaculata opens the gate of heaven to us, as an ancient hymn declares, a hymn in which we find the oldest known mention of Mary's title as Mother of the Church:

> *Virgo Mater Ecclesie*
> *Eterne porta glorie*
> *Ora pro nobis omnibus*
> *Qui tui memoriam agimus.*

> Virgin Mother of the Church,
> Gateway to eternal glory,
> Pray for each and all of us
> Who celebrate your memory.
> (*Manuscript from St. Gall*: n. 390, XII century)

It is easy to understand why the Church founded on the Apostles "admires and glorifies in Mary the most excellent fruit of the Redemption, and joyfully contemplates in her as in an unblemished mirror, what she herself desires and hopes wholly to be"(*Constitution on the Liturgy*, n. 103).

Chapter 7

THE IMMACULATA'S
UNIVERSAL MEDIATION

I F THE VIRGIN MARY WAS CREATED BY GOD AND "FASH-
ioned as a new creature" by the Holy Spirit, it was, as
we have said, so that she might become the mother of
God. Henceforth she lives with the very life of the Holy Spirit,
and together with him is sent on a mission: to complete within
us the efficacious Redemption brought about by our sole Mediator, Jesus.

In a certain sense the definitive glory that Mary enjoys, "carried up to Heaven in body and soul," manifests how perfect
was the Redemption Jesus effected in her. When Christ presents Mary to the Father he hands over to him for eternity the
masterpiece of creation, of human redemption. In Mary who
is glorified, the Church is made perfect. When Christ returns
at the end of ages there will not be a more perfect Church.
But, joined to their Immaculate Mother in the deepest recesses
of her maternal bosom, the countless members of Christ who
have been formed in her by the Holy Spirit will share with her,
each individually and all together, her Son's eternal glory.

Thus to share Mary's glory in heaven, every member of the
Church must on earth share her special grace; without this
universal mediation of Mary the Immaculata it is impossible

for anyone to attain divine life in close intimacy with God, the One in Three.

This mediation of Mary's was, for Father Kolbe, the other pole of his contemplation, the first being her Immaculate Conception. But these two poles are reciprocally related. Here is what he says:

1. Immaculate Conception and Mediation

Everyone knows how closely the various truths of Christian doctrine are intertwined with each other. The dogmas of Catholicism grow out of each other and constantly enrich each other. Here is an example: Basing themselves solely on Catholic doctrine concerning the hypostatic union of the divine and the human in the person of the Word, the Fathers of the Council of Ephesus proclaimed the dogma of Mary's divine maternity.

Once it had been realized what relationships united Jesus with Mary his mother, the Catholic faith was led to conclude that there could be no original sin in the mother of the Savior. No Catholic could have dared to suppose that at any moment of her existence she might have been a slave of Satan.

In the same way, when they considered the important mission confided to the Most Blessed Virgin, and her unspeakably close union with the Holy Spirit (the Immaculate Conception), the faithful were led to place themselves with full confidence under the gentle protection of Mary.

Up to the present our relationship, within the whole scheme of redemption, to Mary, the Co-redemptrix and Dispensatrix of all graces, has not been fully and completely understood. But in our time faith in her mediation grows day by day. We should like to show here how the truth of Mary's mediation is a consequence of the dogma of her Immaculate Conception.

The work of human redemption depends immediately on the second Person of the Trinity, Jesus Christ, who through his blood reconciled us with the Father, who made up for Adam's sin, and merited for us the gift of sanctifying grace and the various actual graces we need, along with the right to heaven.

However, the third Person of the Blessed Trinity also shares in this work. By the power of the redemption wrought by Christ the Holy Spirit transforms the souls of men into temples of God; he makes of us the adoptive children of God and the heirs of the heavenly kingdom, as St. Paul declares:

> But you are washed, but you are sanctified, but you are justified in the name of our Lord Jesus Christ and the Spirit of our God. (1 Cor 6:11)

Penetrating the depths of our souls, the Holy Spirit God-who-is-Love, unites us to the two other divine Persons. So St. Paul writes to the Romans:

> We know not what we should pray for as we ought; but the Spirit himself asks for us with unspeakable groanings. (Rom 8:26)

Similarly, in the first Epistle to the Corinthians we read that the distribution of grace depends on the will of the Holy Spirit:

> The manifestation of the Spirit is given to every man unto profit; to one indeed, by the Spirit is given the word of wisdom; and to another the word of knowledge according to the same Spirit. To another faith in the same Spirit; to another the grace of healing in one Spirit. To another, the working of miracles, to another prophecy, to another the discerning of spirits, to another diverse kinds of tongues, to another interpreta-

tion of speeches. But all of these things one and the same Spirit worketh, dividing to everyone according as he wills. (1 Cor 12:7-11)

Just as the Son, to show us how great his love is, became a man, so too the third Person, God-who-is-Love, willed to show his mediation as regards the Father and the Son by means of a concrete sign. This sign is the heart of the Immaculate Virgin, according to what the saints tell us, especially those who love to consider Mary as the spouse of the Holy Spirit. This was the conclusion drawn by St. Louis de Montfort, in accordance with the teaching of the Fathers. . . . Since the death of Christ, the Holy Spirit acts within us too, by means of Mary. The Creator's word spoken to the serpent about the Immaculata: "She shall crush thy head" (Gn 3:15), must be understood, as the theologians maintain, as applying to all times.

Till the end of the world it will be the task of the Holy Spirit to form the new members predestined to glory in the mystical body of Christ. And as St. de Montfort shows, this task is carried to completion with Mary, in Mary and through Mary.

We are led to this conclusion, namely that the Holy Spirit acts through Mary, by considering various texts of Holy Scripture and the sayings of saints, who are the best interpreters of Holy Writ. "I shall ask the Father, and he will send you another Paraclete, who will abide with you forever, the Spirit of truth" (Jn 14: 16-17). "But the Paraclete, the Holy Spirit whom the Father will send you in my name, he will teach you all truth, and will recall to you all that I have told you" (Jn 14: 26). "When he comes, the Spirit of truth, he will lead you to all truth . . . he will glorify me" (Jn 16:13-14).

Just as the second divine Person appears in his Incarnation as the "seed of the woman," so the Holy Spirit manifests his share in the work of the Redemption through the Immaculate Virgin who, although she is a person entirely distinct from him, is so intimately associated with him that our minds cannot understand it. So, while their union is not of the same order as the hypostatic union linking the human and the divine natures in Christ, it remains true to say that Mary's action is the very action of the Holy Spirit. For Mary as the spouse of the Holy Spirit is raised to such a height of perfection above all other creatures that she accomplishes in everything the will of the Holy Spirit who dwelt in her from the first instant of her conception.

If we consider all these truths together we can conclude that Mary, as Mother of Jesus our Savior, was made the Co-redemptrix of the human race; as the spouse of the Holy Spirit she shares in the distribution of all graces. This is why theologians are justified in saying (following the great tradition of the Fathers): "Even as the first Eve brought ruin upon us by acts which were truly free, a ruin which therefore is attributed to her, so Mary took part in the reparation by her own fully free actions . . . so that one can with certainty speak of a true mediation, in the strict sense of the term."

In these last days especially we contemplate the Immaculata, the spouse of the Holy Spirit, in her role as Mediatrix in our regard.

In 1830 the Most Blessed Virgin appeared to Sister Catherine Laboure. From the account given by this novice we learn the purpose of Mary's appearing: she wished to affirm her Immaculate Conception and her extraordinary power with God. "The Most Blessed Virgin cast her eyes on me and at the same time I heard her voice say: 'The globe of the world represents each and every human being.' Further, she said: 'This is the symbol of the graces which I give to all those who call upon me.' Next I saw an image, oval in shape, which surrounded the figure of the most Blessed Virgin; on it, in golden letters, the following invocation was written: 'O Mary conceived without sin, pray for us who have recourse to thee.' At the same time I heard a voice say: 'Have a medal struck according to this model; all those who wear it will receive many graces.'"

At Lourdes the Immaculate Virgin called on all to do penance; then, to show us so to speak the source whence we would obtain protection, she recited the beads. From that time on, at Lourdes, the Immaculata began to carry out her role as Mediatrix: she invited the sick to come to her; she gathered together the lame and infirm to heal them and to show us how much we depend on her even in our natural life. Tenderly, she drew to herself the spiritually infirm, unbelievers, sinners whose hearts were hardened, she diffused in their souls the grace of supernatural life, to convince them of the power she has to give supernatural life. What is remarkable is that these miracles are performed by Christ in the spot chosen by his Mother.

Everything that has happened at Lourdes through the Most Blessed Virgin illustrates the truth of these words of St. Peter Damian: "by a woman the curse was brought upon the earth, and by a woman a blessing descended upon earth"; and these other words of St. Augustine: "the ruin of mankind came about through the poison injected by a woman; the regeneration of mankind is the salvation brought about through a woman."

What St. Bernard said has been translated into deeds by the Immaculate Virgin: "Such is the will of God, who decreed that we should obtain everything we need through Mary." (*Miles Immaculatae*, I, 1938)

If we insist on these truths: that Mary is the SIGN of the mediation of the Holy Spirit, and the INSTRUMENT in the hands of this second Paraclete sent to us by Christ, we shall be able to grasp all the better the thought of Father Kolbe in the light of the teaching of Vatican II.

2. The Immaculata, Sign of the Holy, Spirit's Mediation

One proves that movement is possible by moving. Instead of harping on theological arguments to prove the possibility of a dogma of Mary's mediation—given the absolute and unique mediation of Jesus—Father Kolbe prefers to stress the fact that such Marian mediation actually takes place.

He begins with a principle which is very simple, and which is based on fact:

> Catholic dogmas grow out of each other and constantly enrich one another.

A few examples will suffice to show how true this principle is.

As regards the mediation of Mary, let us look at the way certain facts follow from each other. Consider how after centuries of theological discussion the dogma of the Immaculate Conception was finally defined, and how it was obviously confirmed at Lourdes by Mary herself, four years later. This opens up a new approach for looking at the question of Mary's mediation, an approach which gives added strength, clarity and precision to the traditional arguments on this topic.

What we mean is this:

By saying "I am the Immaculate Conception," Mary clearly showed that she is intimately united with the third Person of the Trinity whose privileged sanctuary, whose image she is; we can truly say that her life is the very life of the Holy Spirit in her.

Now, the Holy Spirit did not come to the Church only at Pentecost, *after* the Passion, Death and Resurrection of Christ. True, on Pentecost he manifested himself to the Apostles and disciples, thus inaugurating the Church in its members.

But by fashioning the most Blessed Virgin as a new creature,

93

the Holy Spirit from that very instant made her the obvious sign of his personal presence in the world; Mary's Immaculate Conception is also the immaculate conception of the Church. From that very instant, then, the Holy Spirit was sent and given to the world through Mary the Immaculata. By preparing our Lady for her divine maternity he prepared the way for the coming of the Son. Hence, we may say that the Immaculata's life, naturally and supernaturally, is the sign of the living presence of the Holy Spirit in the world.

Once the Son of God had become incarnate in Mary, the Holy Spirit manifested through her in a sensible manner all the wealth of maternal love which he is in God, and which made Mary such a perfect mother, always drawing her closer and closer to her Son. At Cana, the Holy Spirit through Mary provoked the response of Jesus when she said: "They have no more wine"; for Jesus knows full well that everything his mother says and does is inspired by the Spirit of truth and love. So, when Mary told the servants, "Do whatever he tells you," Jesus obeyed the Spirit which thus launched him definitely on the mission which would lead him to Calvary. From that time on he considered his mother as the new Eve associated with himself, the new Adam: "Woman, what is that to me and to thee?" The Most Blessed Virgin did not lose her title as his Mother, but her maternity began reaching ever farther out, becoming the universal motherhood which had been promised in vain to the first Eve.

When the one Savior purifies and justifies all men who are sinners in Adam, the Holy Spirit also purifies and justifies them by giving to the new Eve the whole weight of love that will fill the heart of the new Adam, thus repairing the deadly seduction practiced by the first Eve, who instilled the poison of disobedience into the heart of the first Adam. Christ suffered and died, not in his divinity, but in his humanity. So too the third Person, the Holy Spirit, the Gift of God, does not experience compassion in his divine nature. But what compassion does he not experience in the heart of Mary Immaculate, the Mother of sorrows! Since the union between the Holy Spirit and Mary is so much more than a merely moral union, their compassion reached a depth such that it approximated the infinite degree of divine Love itself.

Father Kolbe does not hesitate to write:

> The Immaculata personifies the mercy of God. (Sketch, 1940)

Intimately associated as she is with Christ suffering and dying, the Virgin is, by the same Spirit, a true mediatrix in the sense in which the Holy Spirit himself is a mediator with regard to the unique Mediator, Jesus Christ. All of us are redeemed by the divine Love which, through the united hearts of the new Adam and of the new Eve, offers reparation to the Father for the sin committed by our first parents, Adam and Eve.

> For just as the Son is the eternal Mediator between the Father and the Holy Spirit (in the divinity itself—the Holy Spirit proceeds from the Father and the Son[1]), so too Jesus the incarnate Son of God becomes the direct Mediator between the Father and the Holy Spirit who, so to speak, is "quasi-incarnate" in the Immaculata, the representative and spiritual Mother of all humanity. (Sketch, 1940)

Here Father Kolbe shows clearly that the most Blessed Virgin is not considered either as a mediatrix or a redeemer *by herself*. She was fashioned by the Holy Spirit because the redemptive act of God's Son had redeemed her in advance, in a most sublime manner, by exempting her from Original Sin; and since as St. Paul teaches, we are purified by Jesus and his Spirit, the Virgin too is created immaculate, totally spotless, in anticipation of the Cross.

But on Calvary this redeemed creature becomes, thanks to her ineffable union with the Holy Spirit, truly a Co-redemptrix.

> As the Mother of Jesus our Savior, Mary was the Coredemptrix of the human race; as the spouse of the Holy Spirit, she shares in the distribution of all graces.

In the Trinity the Spirit urges the Son to give himself in love to the Father; he does the same thing for us, God's adoptive cover with what loving attention our Heavenly Mother watched over each one of us without ceasing, over every soul individually, because all are her children. She strives to shape them after the model, Jesus, her first-born, the archetype of all sanctity, the Man-God. (Sketch, 1940)

It would take too long to cite all Father Kolbe's statements concerning Mary as mediatrix and distributrix of all graces. Here is a resumé of his thinking on the subject, found in a letter to one of his Brothers, who had inquired after the possibility of such mediation.

> The union between the Immaculata and the Holy Spirit is so inexpressible, yet so perfect, that the Holy Spirit acts only by the Most Blessed Virgin, his Spouse. This is why she is the Mediatrix of all grace given by the Holy Spirit. And since every grace is a gift of God the Father through the Son and by the Holy Spirit, it follows that there is no grace which Mary cannot dispose of as her own, which is not given to her for this purpose. (Letter to Father Mikolajezyk, July 25, 1935)

4. Father Kolbe's Doctrine in the Light of Vatican II

When we think of Mary in this fashion, we can follow all the better Father Kolbe's thought concerning the mediation of the most Blessed Virgin. The Second Vatican Council has clearly stated Mary's position with reference to the one Mediator, Christ, her Son. "The Blessed Virgin is invoked in the Church under the titles of 'advocate,' 'helper,' 'mediatrix,' but always in such a way that no derogation from, no addition to the dignity and the efficacy of the one sole Mediator may be implied" (*Lumen Gentium*, n. 62).

It must be admitted that some of the expressions used by Father Kolbe do not seem to have avoided the serious ambiguity common in his time—an ambiguity so keenly felt during the Council when the chapter on the most Blessed Virgin was being drawn up. The notion that Mary is our mediatrix because Christ, the sole Mediator between God and man, established his Mother as a necessary mediatrix between himself and us poor sinners, can indeed be falsely interpreted. It might be supposed that Mary completes the work of our salvation, left more or less unfinished by her Son. Father Kolbe writes:

> Jesus Christ is the sole Mediator between God and humanity; the Immaculata is the unique mediatrix between Jesus and humanity. And we ourselves must become mediators between the Immaculata and the souls dispersed throughout the world. (Letter to the seminarians at Assisi, April 6, 1934)

All he is doing, really, is re-using expressions employed before by St. Louis de Montfort: "Let us say boldly with St. Bernard that we need a mediatrix with the Mediator himself; and that the most Blessed Virgin is certainly the one most fitted to fulfill this charitable role; it was through her that Jesus Christ came to us, and it is through her that we must go to him" (*Treatise on True Devotion to the Blessed Virgin Mary*).

All this series of successive "mediations" undoubtedly looks suspicious to those who, since the Council, perceive more clearly the difference between Jesus, the sole Mediator, and his mother, "our advocate, our helper, our mediatrix."

Of course, Father Kolbe understood perfectly well how one should avoid all error on this point. We must not separate the mediation of Mary from that of the Holy Spirit, the second Paraclete. So, he says that Mary is the manifest sign of the Holy Spirit, and is inseparable from him when she acts as

97

mediatrix; this is something quite obvious to those who, like St. de Montfort, consider Mary as the spouse of the Holy Spirit.

Father Kolbe displays here the acute mind of the theologian and of the saint. He knew that de Montfort, who never heard of the apparitions of the Rue du Bac or of Lourdes, had remained limited to the consideration of a moral bond between Mary and the Holy Spirit. But since it is perfectly possible to understand the union which St. de Montfort writes about, in the meaning it acquired at Lourdes, Father Kolbe does not hesitate to interpret it so.

Further, the liturgy had confirmed this manner of looking at the mediation of Mary with Jesus, as St. de Montfort expressed it; we can see this in the Collect of the former Mass of Mary Mediatrix. Father Kolbe was very familiar with this prayer, since he often said this Mass as a votive Mass.

Put back in their historical context, the affirmations of Father Kolbe should cause no more surprise to anyone. Never does he imagine Mary veiling off Christ from us! On the contrary, he sees her *in the same way* in which Jesus himself presented the Holy Spirit to his Apostles. St. Paul realized perfectly well that if Jesus is indeed the one sole Mediator, the Holy Spirit himself is a Mediator between us and Christ. As we have observed, Father Kolbe insists on this presence of the Holy Spirit, the Spirit of Jesus, which makes Christians live the Christ-life, and which draws them closer to Jesus. "No one can say 'Jesus is the Lord' except through the Holy Spirit" (1 Cor 12: 3). If the Spirit of Jesus does not dwell in us, we cannot recognize Christ, nor can we take him in truth as our one Mediator. Jesus gives us, as coming from the Father, this Third Divine Person to dwell in us as our advocate, our helper, our Mediator. Because Mary is united to the Holy Spirit in such an ineffable manner, she takes part in this intimate mediation of the second Paraclete. Mary does not "block off" either Christ or the Holy Spirit from us.

When we reflect on these two truths: that all graces come from the Father, by the Son and the Holy Spirit and that our holy Mother Mary is, so to speak, one with the Holy Spirit, we are driven to the conclusion that this Most Holy Mother is indeed the intermediary by whom all graces come to us. (Conference, September 25, 1937)

We must then draw this conclusion, so important in the life of every Christian:

Since she is the mediatrix of all graces, it is only in so far as we approach her that we too can become channels of grace, intermediaries of the graces that come from the Father by the Son (who merited them), and through the Immaculata (who distributes them), so that they can flood our souls and through us reach other souls as well. (Letter to the seminarians at Cracow, February 8, 1934)

United with the Immaculata and with the Holy Spirit in the Mystical Body of Christ we should all draw near to her, so as to give ourselves to God, and to give God to others.

This doctrine of Father Kolbe's on the motherly mediation of Mary, carried on inseparably from the Holy Spirit, the second Paraclete, is based on Scripture:

Because she is the mother of Jesus and of his disciples, [says Father Feuillet], Mary is intimately linked with the Holy Spirit. The Holy Spirit himself seems to fulfill a sort of maternal function. A mother is called upon, first of all, to give life by bringing her children into the world. She is further called upon to educate her children, as we have mentioned, and to bring them up to adulthood.

Now, both St. Paul and St. John show us the Holy Spirit fulfilling this double role. He is in the first place the principle of life. To the "letter" of the Old Covenant, which brought death by condemning all guilty ones, the Apostle opposes the Holy Spirit who, in the New Covenant, gives life to men (2 Cor 3:6). On the other hand, St. John tells us "The Spirit gives life; the flesh profits nothing" (Jn 6:63). At baptism, God's new children are born of water and the Holy Spirit (Jn 3:5). There exists a definite relationship between Mary's virginal maternity and the conception of the Son of God in her womb under the action of the Holy Spirit, on the one hand; and on the other, the supernatural birth of Christians by the power of the same Spirit. "Just as," declares St. Thomas, "Christians are spiritually sanctified by the Holy Spirit and become sons of God by adoption, so Christ was conceived in holiness by the Holy Spirit, so as to be the Son of God by nature" (*STH III*, q. 32, a. 1). Let us also recall John's image of "living water," to designate the Holy Spirit. The educative function of the Spirit is no less strongly stressed both in the Fourth Gospel and in St. Paul. In the discourse after the Last Supper (Jn 14-16), the Holy Spirit is presented as the interior teacher; he instructs the soul from within, and helps the disciples to interiorize, so to say, the divine truth brought to them by Jesus, and which he himself actually is, in person. St. Paul, in turn, teaches that it is the Holy Spirit who inspires Christians to adopt the filial sentiments of Jesus, and makes them recognize as their true Father the very Father of Jesus (Rom 8:15-17), somewhat as a mother finds her happiness in making her baby recognize his father and call him by name.

This close relationship between Mary and the Holy Spirit is also brought out by the third and fourth Gospels. In St. Luke's account of the Annunciation, it is the Holy Spirit who, by placing in Mary, so to speak, the germ of the redemptive Incarnation, makes of her the Mother of the Messiah who is also the incarnate Son of God; at the same time he makes her in principle the Mother of the messianic people (since there can be no Messiah without a messianic people). In the closing versicles of St. John's account of the Passion, Jesus begins by entrusting his Mother to his disciple (Jn 19:25-27); then, immediately afterward, he gives us his Spirit by dying for us and "yielding up his Spirit" (Jn 19:28-30). We mentioned above that Jesus consoled his disciples for the privation of his own sensible presence by giving them his own mother. But it is quite obvious from the promises found in John 14-16 that he consoled them above all by the Gift of the Holy Spirit, the Paraclete. These two gifts made by Jesus: that of his own mother, and that of the Holy Spirit, are intimately connected, inseparable from each other; the Spirit is present wherever the action of the Most Blessed Virgin takes place. (*op. cit., pp.* 219-220)

This quotation is like an echo of what Father Kolbe had written:

The Immaculata is so perfect, she is so closely united with the Holy Spirit that she can be called his spouse. For this reason we consecrate everything to her. In her we find everything. She is so to speak the personification of the Holy Spirit. (Conference, June 20, 1937)

Let us not get ahead of our topic. Still, in the history of the development of Catholic dogma, it seems clear that our understanding of Mary's mediation in the order of grace reached its maturity after the Council, in harmony with Father Kolbe's view of the action of the Holy Spirit.

Everything develops and perfects itself with time. We cannot expect that past generations should have grasped the problem of the Immaculate Conception as fully as we do today, after the definition of the dogma. But we must not go backward. (Letter to Niepokalanow)

Mary's affirmation at Lourdes, "I am the Immaculate Conception," had certainly contributed a great deal to provoke the reflections not only of Father Kolbe, but also of Pope Pius XII himself. When celebrating the centenary of the definition of the dogma by Pius IX in 1854, Pius XII did not hesitate to say that Mary at Lourdes had, by her authority as Mother, confirmed the dogma of the Immaculate Conception.

Henceforth, in this clearer understanding of the intimate union between Mary, because she was Immaculate, with the Holy Spirit, and in conformity with the clarifications laid down by the Council, it is easy to understand how the Most Blessed Virgin can be called Mediatrix

> without there resulting from this title any derogation or addition regarding the dignity and efficacy of the one sole Mediator, Christ. (*Lumen Gentium*, n. 62)

ENDNOTES

[1] Even in the divine life of the Trinity, Father Kolbe loves to see the Son as Mediator between the Father and the Holy Spirit.

Chapter 8

THE POWER OF
MARIAN CONSECRATION

ONE REMAINS SURPRISED AT THE DARING THOUGHT AND hopes of Father Kolbe, which aimed at nothing less than the spiritual conquest of the entire world. This apostle had a magnanimous heart indeed. Nothing was too much for the service of God through this sublime creature, the Immaculate Mother of God and our Mother, Queen of heaven and earth.

He was eager to secure the sanctification of individuals, to engage in Christian apostolate under all its forms: the consecration of daily work, the Christianization of the means of social communication—press, publishing, radio, TV, films—not forgetting dialogue with non-believers, and above all the reunion of all Christians.

> The Immaculata must conquer the whole world for herself, and each individual soul as well, so that she can bring all back to God. This is why we must acknowledge her for what she is, and submit to her and to her reign, which is all gentleness.

He wanted to see every person renew his baptismal promises by making an unreserved consecration to the Immaculata, thus making effective his re-birth in baptism.

On Easter Sunday, 1937 Father Kolbe declared:

We were born again in baptism, which washed away our sins. We are reborn incessantly in the Sacrament of Confession. We are called to become like God; and to help us do so we have the most blessed Sacrament. . . . How can we dispose ourselves so as to receive the greatest possible influx of grace? Let us consecrate ourselves to the Immaculata. Let her prepare us herself. Let her receive her Son in us. This is the most perfect means, the one Jesus prefers, and the one that will afford us the most abundant fruits of grace. (Conference, March 28, 1937)

1. His Act of Consecration to the Immaculata

O Immaculata, Queen of heaven and earth, refuge of sinners and our most loving Mother. God has willed to entrust the entire order of mercy to you. I . . . . . a repentant sinner, cast myself at your feet, humbly imploring you to take me, with all that I am and have, wholly to yourself as your property and possession. Please make of me, of all my powers of soul and body, of my whole life, death and eternity whatever most pleases you.

If it pleases you, even use all that I am and have without reserve to accomplish what was written of you: "She will crush (the serpent's) head," and "you alone have destroyed all heresies in the whole world."

Let me be a fit instrument in your immaculate and merciful hands for introducing and increasing your glory to the maximum in all the many strayed and indifferent souls, and thus help extend as far as possible the blessed kingdom of the most Sacred Heart of Jesus. For wherever you enter, you obtain the grace of conversion and growth in holiness, since it is through your hands that all the graces come to us from the most Sacred Heart of Jesus.[1]

Today we can understand more fully the true meaning of this act of consecration written by Father Kolbe in 1917. He spent his life commenting on it, and drawing from it all the richness it contains. The Sacred Heart of Jesus, as a divine reality, is really nothing other than the Holy Spirit, the *"conception" springing forth* from God's inner being, a truly maternal love (See testament-text above, p. 3).

The last commentary on this act of consecration which we possess from his pen was written in 1940; here are its closing lines:

> God sends to us the one who personifies his love: Mary, the spouse of the Spirit—a spirit of maternal love—immaculate, all beautiful, spotless, even though she is our sister, a true daughter of the human race. God confides to her the communication of his mercy to souls. He makes of her the Mediatrix of the graces merited for us by her divine Son, for she is full of grace, the mother of all souls born of grace, reborn, and always being reborn, becoming ever more God-like.

It is not superfluous to point out the essential aspects of this act of consecration.

2. In View of the Kingdom of Christ

At the outset Father Kolbe indicates the fundamental orientation of the act as well as its purpose when he says:

> O Immaculata, Queen of heaven and earth . . .

This consecration aims, in fact, at bringing about the desire Jesus expressed in his sacerdotal prayer; he wants to give us his glory in his kingdom, so that we may be one with him in eternal life. And as he himself says, "eternal life is this: to know thee, the one true God, and Jesus Christ whom thou has sent" (Jn 17:3).

Mary alone can instruct each one of us at every instant, can guide and draw us to herself, so that it may no longer be we but she who lives in us, even as Jesus lives in her, and as the Father lives in the Son. (Letter to the Franciscan students at Cracow, November 8, 1934)

Taken out of context these words would be open to question. But—and all the examination we have been making here shows it—for Father Kolbe the Immaculata is the one who is fully possessed by the Holy Spirit.

God has decided that we should receive everything from the Father, from the Son and from the Holy Spirit, and from the Immaculata. This is the only path that each and every grace can follow. (Conference, July 3, 1938)

In this consecration to the Immaculata, he does not want us merely to contemplate her with our intellects; through our hearts our intellects will enter with the Immaculata into the very mystery of God.

In practice, we know that the souls that have given themselves completely and unrestrictedly to the Immaculata come to understand better the Lord Jesus and the mysteries of God. The Mother of God cannot lead us anywhere except to the Lord Jesus. (Conference, June 20, 1937)

And we well know that:

Our most holy Mother is given to us to help us understand the Holy Spirit better. (Conference, September 25, 1937)

In heaven, close to the Immaculata, we shall achieve the final purpose of the Militia of the Immaculata, i.e. the greatest glory of God through the Immaculata. (Ms 1920, in *Miles Immaculatae*)

3. Belong to the Immaculata

In a letter which he wrote on the ship that was bringing him back to Italy from the Far East, Father Kolbe explained his thought more fully to one of his followers who had asked him to clarify some points in his act of consecration to the Immaculata. The questioner was interested in understanding the link between this consecration and the one promoted by St. Louis de Montfort.

> Any consecration to Mary, including the one proposed by de Montfort, shares the spirit of the Militia of the Immaculata. If anyone wishes to find points where the two seem to differ, he should think over the expression "as your own possession and property." It might be said that de Montfort's expression "slave" implies that one still possesses some personal rights; but this cannot be said of "property." And if there can be found other expressions which go even farther in the direction of self-sacrifice and oblation, such expressions will be all the more in conformity with the spirit of the Militia of the Immaculata. For all these expressions: servant, son, slave, goods, property, are beautiful; but we should like something more; we want to be Mary's totally, without any limitation; so, bringing together all these expressive phrases and others which we might discover we try to sum them all up in one: we wish to "belong totally to the Immaculata." (Letter to Father Vivoda, April 12, 1933)

There we have the best commentary on the following passage in the act of consecration:

> . . . humbly imploring you to take me with all that I am and have wholly to yourself as your possession and property.

In line with this, Father Kolbe declared:

> The ideal of our perfection is our consecration to the Immaculata, always, by day and by night, so that it may not be we who suffer and act, but she through us. (Conference, November 24, 1938)

109

It is because of the affirmation made by Mary at Lourdes that Father Kolbe insists on our giving her not only what we *have* but what we *are*. If Mary says, "I am the Immaculate Conception," it is because her entire being exists only in the pure relationship of a creature with God; she belongs totally to God. One with the Holy Spirit as she is, she is totally consecrated, by all the fibers of her being, to the Father through the Son. Thus she will ever be, throughout eternity; she is in the Son as the Son is in the Father.

If we thus turn over to her everything we have of ourselves, Mary will take our life completely into her hands, to give it to God.

> All of our perfection, all our hope of procuring God's glory depend on our being instruments in the hands of the Immaculata, on being her "things," her property. Such should our interior life be that we become an instrument in her hands, to be guided in everything by her. In truth, we are very weak; and often enough we experience this weakness; the only way to overcome it is to consecrate ourselves to the Immaculata. (Conference, March 9, 1940)

No doubt, Mary is not God; but she is "completely divine," since nothing in her belongs to her. This is why, if we wish to be truly divinized, we must be *totally hers*:

> We must hand ourselves over to the Immaculata; she is totally God's. We must divest ourselves of ourselves, and do it as soon as possible, so as to keep nothing for ourselves, absolutely nothing. She must be the one who acts; let us be her instruments. . . . The main thing is not to act a great deal according to our own ideas, but to place ourselves firmly into her hands. She knows far better than we how to procure the glory of God; by ourselves we could only spoil everything. Everything depends on our perfect docility toward her. There is no greater perfection than the union of our will with hers. (Conference, February 17, 1938)

4. Live by the Immaculata

Man is born again by the waters of Baptism, and becomes in this way a child of God. The water that purifies everything it touches is a symbol of the Immaculata, who purifies everyone who approaches her precisely because she herself is spotless. Everyone who is washed in this water receives the gift of the Holy Spirit, her divine Spouse, who acts only in her and by her. . . .

The new child of God, who has become a member of the "divine family," has God the Father for his father, has the divine Mother for his mother, has the divine Son for his brother. He acquires a divine inheritance by his loving union with the Persons who make up this "divine family." Nor is this all; the divine Son chooses as his spouses the souls to whom he unites himself by this family bond; through him they become the mothers of many other souls. (Sketch, 1940)

It is, then, in a mission of love that the Holy Spirit enlists the most Blessed Virgin to work with him. As this divine Love reaches out particularly towards all men, poor miserable sinners as they are, Father Kolbe is right in saying that God has chosen to confide to Mary the entire order of his mercy.

It follows that our confidence in Mary the Immaculata should be limitless.

Sometimes we ask ourselves, "How can you ever find the courage to become a saint, you who are so weak?" But the weaker we are, the better. The Immaculata is as it were the "incarnation" of divine Mercy. If there is a soul for whom there seems to be no more hope, and if we ask ourselves what is going to happen to it, Mary can lift it to a degree of holiness far beyond that to which it could have ever aspired. Even the weakest, the ones who have strayed farthest, can be rescued by her. You should tell her: "If I am lost and go to hell, others will follow me. But if you stretch

111

out your hand, I could become a great saint and draw many others to Heaven." (Conference, November 24, 1938)

Sometimes we doubt; often enough we have failed to be faithful to grace; and so we think ourselves unworthy to receive God's help. But that is precisely why God has given us our heavenly Mother, to whom he turned over the whole order of his mercy, as though he wished to protect us from his justice. A way has been pointed out to us; and so long as we walk therein we can always obtain God's grace. Never must we say that henceforth grace is beyond our reach.

Even if we have serious sins on our conscience, we can rise again. All we need is to turn to the Immaculata. So, let the sinner who has fallen come to her in full confidence. Don't concentrate your thoughts only on yourself. St. Paul said: "I can do all things in him who strengthens me," and in the same way we can say, "I can do all things, thanks to her who gives me strength." (Conference, August 2, 1938)

Father Kolbe did not say all this in merely abstract terms. His experience enabled him to affirm:

If anyone wishes to contact a President, for instance, or some other high worldly dignitary, he does not go about it by himself; he takes an intermediary with him. The same thing is true when we approach God; let it always be with Mary and through Mary. The saints who became holy most rapidly are the ones who were very zealous in glorifying Mary. We who, compared to them, are so much poorer spiritually, should always take Mary with us on the road to perfection. (Conference, May 30, 1935)

5. Struggle Under the Banner of the Immaculata

The more fully we belong to Mary the Immaculata the more completely will we become like her, become her faithful imitators. St. Paul wrote to his dearly beloved children at Corinth:

"Be ye imitators of me, as I also am of Christ" (1 Cor 11:1). So must we become imitators of the Immaculata, who is herself the most faithful imitator of her Son, through the grace of the Holy Spirit. In this sense, it is permissible for us to say with Father Kolbe:

> Our ideal is that of *unconditional* consecration to the Immaculata, for everything that depends on our will. . . . We have consecrated ourselves to her in this unconditional, unlimited way; and in return she has an obligation to guide us. Our desire, moreover, is not merely that we ourselves should be entirely consecrated to her, but also that all souls all over the world, those now existing and those that will come after us, should likewise consecrate themselves to her unreservedly.
>
> . . . Whoever is truly and totally consecrated to the Immaculata has already reached holiness; and the more perfectly a person lets himself be led by her in the paths of interior and exterior life, the more fully will he share her spirit. (Letter to Fr. Florian Koziura, April 29, 1931)

For this reason we should not be overly preoccupied with our own personal sanctification—even though it is of the highest importance. Our attitude as Christians baptized in Christ's blood ought to be a *missionary*, one; in other words we need to let the devouring fire of Pentecost consume us totally, as it did the Apostles and the Christians who have gone before us.

> Those who give themselves entirely to the Immaculata wish to burn with a love so powerful that it will set fire to everything in their milieu, and cause as many other souls as possible to burn with the same flame. . . . They would wish to conquer the whole world and every soul in particular for the Immaculata, and do this as soon as possible. (Sketch, 1940)

St. Maximilian sees the Church's mission as immense, limit-less. Realizing that this mission is identical with that of the Immaculata, and inseparable from the Spirit of Christ, the Christian will necessarily desire with all his might to be one with his Mother, the Mother of the Church, so that she may make him a true apostle.

> Here is our ideal: to influence our surroundings, to con-quer souls for the Immaculata so that the hearts of our neighbors may open themselves to her, so that she may reign in all hearts everywhere, without distinction of races, nationalities, tongues; so that she may reign in the hearts of all who will live, in all future time, everywhere! (*Knight of the Immaculata*, 1936, p. 227)

The last Council affirmed in striking language that the entire Church is a missionary Church. Not a new truth, of course! But it was the first time that the Church herself, through her official magisterium, had so strongly stressed this determina-tion of the Father and the Son to conquer the world under the leadership of the Holy Spirit, who is like the soul, the spirit of the Church. Following Father Kolbe's lead, we can grasp how impossible it is to separate the Holy Spirit from Mary the Immaculata, since she is the instrument he uses in all he does in the order of grace.

Every real missionary is, in the Church, a real militant as Father Kolbe understood it; this was why he created his *Mili-tia of the Immaculata* so that each member might be a kind of knight of our Lady.

> We have to win the universe and each individual soul, now and in the future, down to the end of time, for the Immaculata, and by her for the Sacred Heart of Jesus. Further, we must be on the watch so that nobody tears any soul away from its consecration to the Immaculata; we should strive rather that souls may constantly deepen their

love for her; that the bond of love between her and these souls may grow ever closer, and that these souls may henceforth be one with her, with her alone. This is how the Immaculata is able to live and love and act in these souls, and through them.

For just as the Immaculata herself belongs to Jesus and to God, so too every soul through her and in her will belong to Jesus and to God in a much more perfect way than would have been possible without her. Such souls will come to love the Sacred Heart of Jesus much better than they have ever done up to now. Like Mary herself, they will come to penetrate into the very depths of love, to understand the cross, the Eucharist much better than before. Through her divine love will set the world on fire and will consume it; then will the "assumption of souls in love" take place. When, oh when will the divinisation of the world in her and through her come about? . . .

For this it is necessary that she and she alone should act, and that those who give themselves to her should do so without restrictions; they must first belong to her; they must plumb the limitless depths of this donation; they must ever strive to draw tighter and tighter this bond of love which penetrates their souls. This is the absolutely indispensable condition. She will act through them in so far as they belong to her. Hence there must remain nothing in them that is theirs; they must he hers totally. (Personal notes, April 23, 1933)

Faithful to the ideal of his father, St. Francis of Assisi, St. Maximilian lived what he taught. All his being was fully consecrated to Mary the Immaculata, even to the supreme sacrifice. When his executioner, Fritch, asked him, "Who are you?" he simply replied: A Catholic priest.

Perhaps he was thinking of the most Blessed Virgin's reply at Lourdes, which revealed her identity: "I am the Immaculate Conception." He too wished to be made divine, by not retaining anything of himself, but being totally immersed in Jesus, the sovereign Priest, through the Immaculata. Thus, like Christ, at once Priest and Victim, Maximilian Kolbe in that instant was indeed the Christ dying and offering himself to his Father on the cross.

And to show the world that God and the Immaculata had accepted his sacrifice, his body was reduced to ashes on Assumption day, August 15, 1941. For eternity he is all God's, in the Immaculata.

Corbara, September 12, 1974
Feast of the Holy Name of Mary

ENDNOTES

[1] St. Maximilian composed this formula in 1917 for the Militia of the Immaculata, which he founded.—Ed.

PAPAL ADDRESSES CONCERNING ST. MAXIMILIAN

October 14, 1971
Press Conference of Cardinal Karol Wojtyla

Cardinal Karol Wojtyla, Archbishop of Cracow (and later Pope John Paul II), in whose diocese the death-camp of Auschwitz (Oswiecim) was located, made the following presentation on October 14, 1971, at the Holy See's press office. He introduced to the reporters this priest, Father Kolbe, who followed Jesus Christ "all the way," and after whose death the extermination camp at Auschwitz lost some of its hellish character.

M AXIMILIAM KOLBE, A FRANCISCAN RELIGIOUS, HAS aroused the attention of the entire world by the sacrifice of his life, which he lovingly offered in favor of an unknown fellow prisoner, the father of a family, who had been picked out, along with nine other prisoners, to die of hunger and thirst in reprisal for the escape of another prisoner. This man, named Gajowniczek, is in Rome today and will be present at the glorification of the man thanks to whom he succeeded in surviving the hell of the concentration camp.

Barely thirty years separate us from the day, the eve of the

Assumption, 1941, on which Father Kolbe, the last survivor of the condemned group, was finally killed by an injection of phenol. Like those of millions of other victims his body was consigned for cremation to one of the ovens which, at Auschwitz, burned day and night. Thus was his wish fulfilled, a longing he had so often expressed: "I would like for my ashes to be dispersed to the four winds...." Little did he imagine that his desire would be so literally fulfilled; but neither did he foresee that, far from making him disappear "without a trace," his humble desire would draw down on him the attention of the whole Church. Rarely has there appeared such unanimity concerning a person's reputation for sanctity.

Father Kolbe's Reply to Those Priests Who Question Their Own Identity

With growing insistence the question arises: "Why Father Kolbe?" Were there not in these death camps other prisoners who bore witness of their love of their fellow men, even to a heroic degree? One thinks of the Polish Bishop, Msgr. Kozal, who literally let himself starve to death because he gave away to his unfortunate companions all his own meagre rations. If we observe the signs of the times, what, we may ask, does the Church mean to tell us by proposing this priest to us today as a model?

Note this well: this man of 47 who had fulfilled with such exemplary fidelity the ideal of St. Francis, wished to die AS A PRIEST. When Fritch, the brutal camp commandant, taken aback by the courage of this prisoner who offered to replace a man condemned to die, asked him: "Who are you?" Maximilian Kolbe simply replied: "A Catholic priest."

So it was as a priest that he accompanied the group of nine miserable men condemned to perish. For his task was not merely to save the tenth one; he had to help the nine others die as Christians. As soon as the fatal door clanged shut behind the

120

condemned men he took charge of them all; and not of them only, but also of all the others dying of hunger in the neighboring bunkers, whose animal-like howls struck terror in the hearts of all who heard them. From the moment Father Kolbe appeared in their midst these wretches felt that they had a protector and helper; and the cells in which they awaited the inexorable denouement thenceforth reechoed with prayers and hymns. The jailers themselves were unnerved by it. "*So was haben wir nie gesehen!*" ("We have never seen the like!") they exclaimed. We shall never know, till judgment day, whether among them there were any "good thieves," converted perhaps at their last hour, by this heroic example they had witnessed. The fact is, and all the survivors of Auschwitz know it, that from Assumption day, 1941, on, the camp became a somewhat less hellish place.

At a time when so many priests all over the world question their identity as priests, Maximilian Kolbe stands before them to give his answer, not with fine-spun theological disquisitions, but with the testimony of his life and of his death. It was enough for him to be like his Master, by bearing witness to a "greater love," the evangelical test that shows now surely one belongs to Christ. Heroism like his is certainly not within the grasp of everyone; but to give up striving for it would spell failure indeed. The answers to the questions that assail us and cause us anguish may well be found in an effort to "go up higher," and we can be sure that grace will provide what nature by itself cannot attain to.

In the Hellish Circle of Hatred

Father Maximilian died in an era characterized by man's fury and scorn for man, in which man was cut down to the level of a robot, a state worse than slavery. The ghastly memory of hell that every concentration camp was is fading little by little, today's young people hardly know anything about it; and history books record facts which the imagination has a hard time picturing. Still, those who survived this period know how horribly, under a totalitarian regime, the human person was degraded, humiliated, despised. In this poisoned soil nothing but hatred could grow. One prisoner wrote: "Ah!, how I hate them all! They have taught me how to hate."

Now, the unheard-of-fact, corroborated by any number of witnesses, is that Maximilian Kolbe did not know what hatred was. Whether in the prison at Pawiak in Warsaw, or behind the barbed wire fence at Auschwitz, he looked with the same clear-sighted vision on executioners and victims alike, so much so that some of the more sadistic among the former could not face his gaze. "Don't look at us like that!" they barked at him. This man, who had become a mere number, 16,670, had won the most arduous of all victories, the victory of love which forgives and pardons. He broke through the infernal circle of hate's dialectic with a heart full of love, and at once the hellish spell was exorcized, and love showed itself stronger than death. Is his witness not strikingly relevant in times like these, when love is so often stretched out on a cross, so often cleft in twain? How few people there are nowadays whose brotherly love does not admit of some form of segregation . . . by race, or nation, or ideology!

A Precursor in the Use of Mass Media

Maximilian Kolbe was also a pioneer in a domain to which attention has been called by one of the pastoral documents of Vatican II, the mass media. He started with nothing; he braved the disapproval of those who looked askance on religious engaged in the apostolate of the press. This man with his poor health, (he had only one-fourth of a lung!) succeeded in starting his "little blue magazine" which by 1939 had nearly a million subscribers, and a newspaper of very modest appearance destined for ordinary folk, peasants and working people. Today we can see that his labors in this field prepared Poland for the bloody trial awaiting her, a trial which cost her over six million dead during the second World War. Father Kolbe, a man who took the beatitudes seriously, turned first of all toward the "poor servants of Yahweh," the "*anawim*," who hungered for the word of God even more than for bread. To serve them he wanted to make use of all the resources of technology, all the latest conquests of progress. In 1938 he inaugurated a broadcasting station, and gave serious thought to creating an airport at Niepokalanow, the "city of the Immaculata." When a group of prelates, somewhat shocked by all these "wild projects" of his asked him, "What would St. Francis be doing in your place?" he replied without batting an eyelash: "He would roll up his sleeves and set to work with us!" As he saw it, the "Canticle of Creatures" included the huge rotary presses and the linotype machines; and the 600 Brothers at Niepokalanow made them sing a song of praise to the glory of God. In the writings of Father Kolbe one could find all the elements needed for a theology of work, the horizontal dimensions of which imply the vertical dimension, the fruitful tension of the Cross

A Precursor of Vatican II's Marian Theology

This man whose ambitions were as vast as the universe—did he not adopt as his own St. Francis of Assisi's words: "*Vorrei mandarvi tutti in paradiso*" ("I should like to send all of you to Paradise"); this missionary who established in Japan his apostolate of the press, wished to bear witness by his life and death to his love for our Lady whom he invoked under her title of the Immaculate Conception. His Marian theology possesses a doctrinal accuracy that enchants those familiar with that keystone of Vatican II, the Constitution on the Church, *Lumen Gentium*. One is tempted to say that he had foreseen, even in its wording, the admirable eighth chapter consecrated to the Virgin Mary. The spiritual fecundity of this humble religious,

123

who was not only a marvel of efficiency—something that our technocratic world appreciates—but also one of the greatest contemplatives of our time, bears witness before the entire world to the unique role played by the Virgin Mother of God. Mother of the Head, she is also the mother of his Body the Church: Christ "spread out and communicated" as Bossuet calls it.

Father Kolbe Invites Us to Take a Stand

It is not by mere chance, it is indeed a sign of the times, that this priest who died in 1941, at the age of 47, in the starvation bunker at Auschwitz, should be beatified during the present Synod whose special purpose was to define more specifically the meaning of the priestly ministry. To the more or less abstract questions asked, he gives a concrete answer, this man of flesh and blood, who was not content himself with mouthing fine phrases, but who went "all the way" in his fidelity to his obligations, who gave blood for blood. We have been questioning him; but in reality it is he who challenges us, calling on us to take a stand and to live up to it. It is not enough to admire him in Bernini's "gloria." We must ask him, in the secret of our own hearts, what he has to tell us, each one of us, personally.

October 17, 1971
Beatification Homily of Pope Paul VI

W<small>HO IS</small> M<small>AXIMILIAN</small> K<small>OLBE</small>? <small>YOU KNOW THE ANSWER;</small> you know him well. So close is he to our generation, to the happenings we have all experienced in our time, that we all know about him. Few other processes of beatification have been conducted amidst such a wealth of information. Solely because we wish to show ourselves concerned with historical truth today, we shall present first of all a biographical sketch of Father Kolbe, written by someone who has studied him very carefully.

The Life of the New Blessed

Father Maximilian Kolbe was born at Zdunska Wola, near Lodz, on January 8, 1894. In 1907 he entered the seminary of the Friars Minor Conventual, and later was sent to Rome where he continued his ecclesiastical studies at the Pontifical Gregorian University and at the Franciscan Seraphicum. While still a student he founded the Militia lmmaculatae. After his ordination on April 28, 1918, he returned to Poland and initiated his Marian apostolate, launching a monthly review *The Knight of the Immaculata*, which by 1938 reached a circulation of nearly a million.

In 1927 he founded Niepokalanow, "the City of the Immaculata," a center for religious life and for various types of apostolate. In 1930 he set out for Japan, where he established a similar center. After returning permanently to Poland, he dedicated himself entirely to the task of publishing various religious periodicals. The second World War found him at the head of the biggest publishing concern in Poland. On September 19, 1939, he was arrested by the Gestapo and deported first to Lamdorf, Germany, and then to the concentration camp of Amtitz. Released on December 8, 1939, he returned to Niepokalanow, and took up anew his interrupted activities. Arrested again in 1941, he was incarcerated in the prison of Pawiak, at Warsaw, then sent off to the concentration camp at Oswiecim (Auschwitz). Having offered to take the place of an unknown fellow prisoner who had been condemned to death in reprisal for the escape of another prisoner, he was consigned to a bunker there to die of starvation.

On August 14, 1941 he was put to death by being given an injection of poison. It was the eve of the Assumption. Thus did he yield up his beautiful soul to God, after having helped and consoled his fellow sufferers. His body, like theirs, was burnt. (Fr. Ernesto Piacentini, OFM CONV.)

His Veneration of the Immaculate Conception

Maximilian Kolbe was an apostle of the formal veneration of Mary seen in all her pristine splendor, in the original and privileged character of the definition she gave of herself at Lourdes: the Immaculate Conception. It is impossible to separate the name of Father Kolbe, his activity or his mission, from the name of Mary Immaculate. He founded the *Militia Immaculatae* here in Rome before he was even a priest, on October 16, 1917; today we may celebrate the anniversary of that occasion. We all know how this humble, meek Franciscan, with incredible courage and extraordinary talent for organization, developed this initiative of his, and made of the devotion to the Mother of Christ, the Woman clothed with the sun, the center of his spirituality, his apostolate and his theology. Let us not be reluctant to admire him, to adopt the watchword which the new Blessed leaves us as his legacy, as though we feared that such zeal to honor Mary might clash with the other two theological and spiritual currents so prominent in today's religious thought and life: the Christological trend, and the ecclesiological trend. No competition here! In Father Kolbe's mind, Christ occupies not merely the first place, but strictly speaking, the only place necessary and sufficient for salvation. Nor is love for the Church and for her mission absent from the teaching or the apostolic endeavors of our new Blessed. For it is precisely from the way Mary completes and serves the universal plan of Christ for the salvation of all men that she draws all her prerogatives and all her greatness.

All this we know very well. Father Kolbe, in total accord with the teaching, the liturgy and the spirituality of the Church, sees Mary as part of the divine plan. In this vision she is the "boundary fixed by eternal counsel," the woman who is "full of grace," the seat of wisdom, the one predestined to be Mother of Christ and queen of the messianic kingdom. At the same time she is the handmaid of the Lord, the woman chosen to offer for the Incarnation of the Word her irreplaceable cooperation, the Mother of the God-man, our Savior. "Mary is the one by whom men reach Jesus, and the one by whom Jesus comes down to men" (L. Bouyer, *Le Trone de la Sagesse*, p. 69).

We must not, then, reproach either the new Blessed or the Church with excessive enthusiasm for the formal religious veneration of Mary. This enthusiasm will never be too great, considering the merits and benefits such veneration provides, precisely because of the mystery of Mary's communion with Christ, expressed so poignantly in the New Testament. No need to fear that it will develop into some sort of "Mariolatry"; for just as the sun will never be out-shone by the moon, neither will the mission of salvation confided to the Church ever be threatened because the Church honors Mary as her exceptional daughter and her spiritual mother. The characteristic aspect of the devotion, of the "hyperdulia" paid by Father Kolbe to Mary (an aspect which is not at all original with him), lies in the importance which, faced with the pressing needs of the Church today, he attaches to her prophecy about the glory of the Lord and the exaltation of the humble, to the power of her intercession, to her marvelous example, to the reality of her maternal love. The Council has confirmed our certitude in regard to all this; and today from high heaven Father Kolbe instructs us and helps us to meditate on all these truths, and to live by them.

This Marian aspect of the sanctity of the new Blessed ranks him among the greatest saints and the far-seeing visionaries who understood, venerated and sang of the mystery of Mary.

A Ray of Light in a Sombre Page of History

Let us now speak of the tragic yet sublime conclusion of Maximilian Kolbe's innocent and zealous life. It is this mainly which leads the Church on this day to honor this humble, gentle, religious man, this active and exemplary son of St. Francis, this knight of the Immaculata. His death is so horrible, so soul-shattering, that we would prefer not to speak of it, never to have to think of it again, so as not to remind Ourselves of the depths to which human vileness can sink when men consider it a sign of superiority and a cause for boasting to show icy cruelty towards defenseless human beings reduced to a state worse than slavery, destined for liquidation! How many millions were thus sacrificed to pride of power and racist folly!

Yet we must remind ourselves of these sombre facts in order to discern among them, here and there, some few traces of human feeling. History, alas! can never forget this frightful page; but in the midst of so much horror she cannot fail to point out too the rays of light which contrast all the more strongly with the surrounding darkness, even while they vanquish it. One of these rays of light, perhaps the most luminous, we see in the emaciated yet tranquil face of Maximilian Kolbe, this hero who never lost his paradoxical, yet well-justified confidence. His name can never perish; he serves as a reminder of the well-springs of moral courage that could still be found among these wretched men, a prey to terror and despair. In this dreadful antechamber of death a divine and imperishable word of life echoes—the word spoken by Jesus revealing to us the secret of why the innocent suffer; it led him to expiate, to be a victim, a sacrifice of love. "Greater love than this no man hath, that a man lay down his life for his friends" (Jn 15:13). Jesus was speaking of himself, a few hours before he sacrificed himself for man's salvation. All men are Jesus' friends if they listen to his word. In the terrible death camp of Auschwitz Father Kolbe exemplified this redemptive love in two ways.

Father Kolbe's Lesson to Us in the Midst of Today's Questioning of the Priesthood

Which of us does not remember this extraordinary story? "I am a Catholic priest," he said, when he offered himself to die in another man's place, knowing what kind of death it would be! He replaced one of his companions in misery who was unknown to him, and who had already been picked out for the blind act of revenge. What a magnificent moment! His offer was accepted. It rose from a heart so long accustomed to self-sacrifice that it had become natural and spontaneous to him, a logical consequence of his priesthood. For is the priest not another Christ? Was not Christ both the Priest and the Victim

129

who redeemed the human race? What a glory it is for us priests, and what a lesson, to find in Blessed Maximilian such a splendid exemplification of our consecration and of our mission! What a warning he addresses to us in this hour of uncertainty, when at times human nature would like to assert its claims to the detriment of our supernatural vocation which calls us to the total donation of ourselves to Christ, which demands that we follow him! What a consolation it must be for all good and faithful priests and religious, so dear to Our heart, who, filled with the legitimate and praiseworthy desire to transcend personal mediocrity and social frustration, understand their mission just as he did. "I am a Catholic priest"—and for this reason I offer my life to save those of others. Such would seem to be the watchword which the new Blessed leaves especially to us, ministers of God's Church, and likewise to all those who accept his spirit.

A Son of the Noble Polish Nation

To this priestly aspect we can add another, which shows the deep affection that motivated Blessed Maximilian's sacrifice: he was a true Pole. Because of this he was condemned to the concentration camp; and as a Polish patriot he was willing to give up his life for that of a fellow countryman, Francis Gajowniczek. How much is suggested by this human social and ethnic aspect of the freely-chosen death of Maximilian Kolbe, a son of the noble, Catholic, Polish nation! It seems to us that this heroic act of his exemplifies in typical fashion the historic destiny of his nation; for suffering is the centuries-old vocation of the Polish people. It has learned how to find in the trials that afflict its national life the consciousness of its unity; its chivalrous mission to achieve liberty through the pride of its sons' and daughters' spontaneous sacrifice, and their readiness to give themselves for each other as they rise above their vivacity in unconquered concord; its indelible Catholic character which makes of it a living and suffering member of the universal Church; its firm conviction that the secret of its restoration will be found in Mary's marvelous protection. These rays of light issuing from the new Polish martyr show us the true visage of his country. Let us ask this typical Polish hero to give us his firmness in the faith, his ardor in charity, the blessings of concord, prosperity and peace to all his people. The Church and the whole world will rejoice over it together!

Why We Call Him "Blessed"

[The following paragraphs were actually the pastoral introduction to the Pope's homily. Because of the different purposes of this book they have been placed here as a fitting conclusion.]

So Maximilian Kolbe is called "Blessed." What does this title mean? It means that the Church recognizes him as an exceptional figure, a man in whom the grace of God and his own soul have so come together as to produce a stupendous life. Whoever examines his life carefully, discovers this close union of the divine and the human operating as a dual principle. One is mysterious, the other can be experienced; one is transcendent but interior, the other natural but complex and expanded, so that it reaches that extraordinary image of the moral and spiritual greatness we call holiness; that is perfection in the religious sphere, a sphere that soars towards the infinite heights of the Absolute, as you know. The title "Blessed" therefore means a person is worthy of that formal religious veneration permitted in the places and among the groups with whom he was associated, a veneration that implies admiration of the person receiving it because of the unusual and magnificent way he reflects the sanctifying Spirit. This title means the person is saved and glorious. It means he is a citizen of heaven with all the particular marks that identify a citizen of earth. It means he

131

is a brother and friend who we know is still one of us, now more than ever, because now he is identified as an active member of the communion of Saints, which is that mystical body of Christ, the Church, which lives both in time and in eternity.

This title means that he is our intercessor therefore, and our protector in the kingdom of charity, together with Christ "who lives forever to make intercession for us" (Heb 7:25). It means, finally, that he is a prize exemplar, the type of person on whom we can base our way of life, since as a "Blessed" he has the privilege of saying to the Christian people with the apostle Paul: "Be imitators of me, as I am of Christ" (1 Cor 4:16; 11:1, etc.).

In this way, then, from this day on, we can look up to Maximilian Kolbe, our new Blessed.

June 7, 1979
Homily at Auschwitz
Pope John Paul II

"THIS IS THE VICTORY THAT OVERCOMES THE WORLD, our faith" (1 Jn 5:4). These words from the letter of St. John come to my mind and enter my heart as I find myself in this place in which a special victory was won through faith, through the faith that gives rise to love of God and of one's neighbor, the unique love, the supreme love that is ready to "lay down (one's) life for (one's) friends" (Jn 15:13, cf. 10:11). A victory, therefore, through love enlivened by faith to the extreme point of the final definitive witness.

This victory through faith and love was won in this place by a man whose first name is Maximilian Mary. Surname: Kolbe. Profession (as registered in the books of the concentration camp): Catholic priest. Vocation: a son of St. Francis. Birth: a son of simple, hard-working, devout parents, who were weavers near Lodz, Poland. By God's grace and the Church's judgment: blessed.

The victory through faith and love was won by him in this

place, which was built for the negation of faith—faith in God and faith in man—and to trample radically not only on love but on all signs of human dignity, of humanity. A place built on hatred and on contempt for man in the name of a crazed ideology. A place built on cruelty. On the entrance gate which still exists, is placed the inscription "*Arbeit Macht Frei*" (Freedom Through Work), which has a sardonic sound, since its meaning was radically contradicted by what took place within.

In this site of the terrible slaughter that brought death to four million people of different nations, Father Maximilian voluntarily offered himself for death in the hunger bunker for a brother and so won a spiritual victory like that of Christ himself. This brother still lives today in the land of Poland.

But was Father Maximilian Kolbe the only one? Certainly he won a victory that was immediately felt by his companions in captivity and is still felt today by the church and the world. However, there is no doubt that many other similar victories were won. I am thinking, for example, of the death in the gas chamber of a concentration camp of the Carmelite Sister Benedicta of the Cross, whose name in the world was Edith Stein, who was an illustrious pupil of Husserl and became one of the glories of contemporary German philosophy, and who was a descendant of a Jewish family living in Wroclaw.

The dignity of man was so horribly trampled on. Victory was won through faith and love.

Can it still be a surprise to anyone that the pope born and brought up in this land, the pope who came to the See of St. Peter from the diocese in whose territory is situated the camp of Oswiecim (Auschwitz), should have begun this first encyclical with the words "*redemptor hominis*" and should have dedicated it as a whole to the cause of man, to the dignity of man, to the threats to him, and finally to his inalienable rights that can so easily be trampled on and annihilated by his fellow men? Is it enough to put man in a different uniform, arm him with the apparatus of violence? Is it enough to impose on him an ideology in which human rights are subjected to the demands of the system, completely subjected to them, so as in practice not to exist at all?

2) I am here today as a pilgrim. It is well known that I have been here many times. So many times. And many times I have gone down to Maximilian Kolbe's death cell and stopped in front of the execution wall and passed among the ruins of the cremation furnaces of Brzezinka (Birkenau). It was impossible for me not to come here as pope.

I have come then to this special shrine, the birthplace, I can say, of the patron of our difficult century, just as nine centuries ago Skalka was the place of the birth under the sword of St. Stanislaus, patron of the Poles.

I have come to pray, I have come to pray with all of you who come here today and with the whole of Poland and the whole of Europe. Christ wishes that I who have become the successor of Peter should give witness before the world to what constitutes the greatness and the misery of contemporary man, to what is his defeat and his victory.

I have come and I kneel on this Golgotha of the modern world, on these tombs, largely nameless like the great Tomb of the Unknown soldier. I kneel before all the inscriptions that come one after another bearing the memory of the victims of Oswiecim in the languages: Polish, English, Bulgarian, Romany, Czech, Danish, French, Greek, Hebrew, Yiddish, Spanish, Flemish, Serbo-Croat, German, Norwegian, Russian, Romanian, Hungarian and Italian.

In particular I pause with you, dear participants in this encounter, before the inscription in Hebrew. This inscription awakens the memory of the people whose sons and daughters were intended for total extermination. This people draws its origin from Abraham, our father in faith (cf. Rm 4:12), as was expressed by Paul of Tarsus. The very people who received from God the commandment "thou shalt not kill" itself experienced in a special measure what is meant by killing. It is not permissible for anyone to pass by this inscription with indifference.

Finally, the last inscription: that in Polish. Six million Poles lost their lives during the Second World War: a fifth of the nation. Yet another stage in the centuries-old fight of this nation, my nation, for its fundamental rights among the peoples of Europe. Yet another loud cry for the right to a place of its own on the map of Europe. Yet another painful reckoning with the conscience of mankind.

Oswiecim is such a reckoning. It is impossible merely to visit it. It is necessary on this occasion to think with fear of how far hatred can go, how far man's destruction of man can go, how far cruelty can go.

Oswiecim is a testimony of war. War brings with it a disproportionate growth of hatred, destruction and cruelty. It cannot be denied that it also manifests new capabilities of human courage, heroism and patriotism, but the fact remains that it is the reckoning of the losses that prevails. That reckoning prevails more and more, since each day sees an increase in the destructive capacity of the weapons invented by modern technology. Not only those who directly bring wars about are responsible for them, but also those who fail to do all they can to prevent them. Therefore I would like to repeat in this place the words that Paul VI pronounced before the United Nations organization:

"It is enough to remember that the blood of millions of men, numberless and unprecedented sufferings, useless slaughter and frightful ruin are the sanction of the covenant which unites you in a solemn pledge which must change the future history of the world: no more war, war never again. It is peace, peace which must guide the destinies of the peoples and of all mankind" (*AAS*, 57, 1965, p. 881).

136

If, however, Oswiecim's great call and the cry of man tortured here is to bear fruit for Europe, and for the world also, the Declaration of Human Rights must have all its just consequences drawn from it, as John XXIII urged in the encyclical *Pacem in Terris.* For the declaration is "a solemn recognition of the personal dignity of every human being, an assertion of everyone's right to be free to seek out the truth, to follow moral principles, discharge the duties imposed by justice, and lead a fully human life. It also recognized other rights connected with these" (John XXIII, *Pacem in Terris,* IV—*AAS* 55, 1963, pp. 295-296). There must be a return to the wisdom of the old teacher Pawel Wlodkowic, rector of the Jagiellonian University of Cracow, and the rights of nations must be ensured; their right to existence, to freedom, to independence, to their own culture and to honorable development. Wlodkowic wrote: "Where power is more at work than love, people seek their own interests and not those of Jesus Christ and accordingly they easily depart from the rule of God's law . . . All the kinds of law are against those who threaten people wishing to live in peace: against them is the civil law . . . the canon law . . . the natural law . . . expressed in the principle 'do to others what you would have done to you.' Against them is the divine law, in that . . . the commandment 'Thou shalt not steal' forbids all robbery and that commandment 'Thou shalt not kill' forbids all violence" (Pawel Wlodkowic, *Saevientibus* (1415), tract II *Solutio Quaest.* 4A, cf. L. Ehrlich, *Pisma Wybrane Pala Wlodkowica,* Warzawa 1968, T.L.S. 61, 58-59).

Never one at the other's expense, at the cost of the enslavement of the other, at the cost of conquest, outrage, exploitation and death.

The one who is speaking these words is the successor of John XXIII and Paul VI. But he is also the son of a nation that in its history has suffered many afflictions from others.

I say this not to accuse but to remind. I am speaking in the name of all the nations whose rights are being violated and forgotten. I am saying it because I am urged to do so by the truth and by solicitude for man.

3) Holy is God! Holy and strong! Holy Immortal One!
From plague, from famine, from fire and from war,
And from war, deliver us, Lord.
Amen.

October 18, 1981
Papal Address to the National Congress of the Militia of the Immaculata
Pope John Paul II, Rome

B ELOVED IN CHRIST! THE REASON THAT MOVED YOU TO ask for this special audience is the commemoration of the fortieth anniversary of the death of Blessed Maximilian Mary Kolbe and of the tenth anniversary of his beatification. You belong, in fact, to the "Militia of Mary Immaculate," founded by him, and you have wished to celebrate these two important and meaningful dates by meeting with the Pope.

And, as you can imagine, I am really happy to welcome you with all the affection and warmth of my heart, because of the beauty and greatness of the ideal that you are trying to live, following the example and teaching of Fr. Maximilian Kolbe, an illustrious son of my country, Poland, a fascinating example with his intelligence and his holiness.

I address my warm greeting, therefore, to the Minister General of the Friars Minor Conventuals, to the superiors and religious, and to all of you, each one in particular, who represent the many nuclei of the "Militia" scattered all over the world. I greet you and I thank you for having come to Rome, where on October 16, 1917, Father Maximilian, as you know, founded the Militia of Mary Immaculate.

I think you above all for wishing to commemorate here with me the dates of his death and beatification, which arouse in me a wave of memories and emotion. How often, in fact, have I gone on pilgrimage to that place of torture and glory, to the "bunker of hunger," in the Auschwitz camp, where he died on August 14, forty years ago, the victim of hatred, but at the same time the victor with his love! And how I remember my last visit, on June 7, 1979, during the journey in Poland, when, entering the haunting room, I knelt at that "Golgotha of the modern world." You also make me remember with intense nostalgia the solemn day of his beatification, on October 17, 1971, when I was around the altar with the Holy Father Paul VI and Cardinal Stefan Wyszynski, and the visit paid on February 26 of this year to the City of Mary Immaculate at Nagasaki, which he founded.

Remembering these dates, we seem to see among us the person of Father Maximilian, serious and stern, affable and smiling; and again we hear Paul VI's eulogy of him in the memorable beatification homily: "Blessed means safe and glorious. It means a citizen of heaven, with all the peculiar signs of the citizen of the earth; it means a brother and friend, whom we know is still ours, in fact, more than ever ours . . . ; it means an advocate and protector in the kingdom of charity; finally, it means an exemplary model, a type of man, to whom we can adapt our art of living. . . ." (*Insegnamenti di Paolo VI*, IX, 1971, p. 906). Paul VI himself mentioned Father Maximilian again in the apostolic letter *Gaudete in Domino* (May 22, 1975) as "A luminous image for our generation . . . a genuine disciple of St. Francis."

Before such an elect example, which is also, however, so human and close to us, reflection becomes more personal and more responsible for you, who belong to the Militia of Mary Immaculate.

The Statutes, approved in their updated form on November 8, 1974, affirm that the association "wishes to extend as much as possible the very gentle Kingdom of the Sacred Heart of Jesus through Mary Immaculate, or rather to be in the service of Mary Immaculate in this mission that she has as Mother of the Church."

This was Father Maximilian's ideal, to which he dedicated his life, intellectual talents, physical strength and tireless activity. Membership in the Militia means complete dedication to the Kingdom of God and to the salvation of souls through Mary Immaculate.

I exhort you therefore to live this ideal of yours with more and more fervent commitment. In our society, your consecration to Mary Immaculate must make you serene, confident and courageous witnesses. Like Father Maximilian you are passionately in love with truth. The Church today essentially needs unity in truth. In fact, it is truth that gives the courage for great decisions, heroic choices, definitive dedication. It is truth that gives the strength to live difficult virtues, the evangelical beatitudes, youthful purity, and consecrated and conjugal chastity! It is knowledge and love of truth which gives rise to priestly, religious and missionary vocations and which moves to charity, to the extent of self-sacrifice, as Father Maximilian did! And the truth is Christ known, followed and witnessed: "I am the light of the world" (Jn 8:12), the Divine Master said, and he added: "You are the light of thw world" (Mt 5:14). The two affirmations are equivalent, clearly laying down the line of conduct and responsibility of every Christian: "He who follows me will not walk in darkness" (Jn 8:12, 12:46).

From truth there logically springs the aspiration to holiness, which was Father Maximilian's supreme ideal. So he wrote: "It is not pride to want to be as holy as possible and to sanctify as many souls as possible, trusting solely in God, through Mary Immaculate" (*Gli scritti di Massimiliano Kolbe, Citta di Vita*, Fireze 1978, Vol. II, p. 715). From truth springs the sense of complete trust and surrender to the Almighty, especially in the tribulations and turmoil that accompany human history.

Beloved in Christ! Be strong in faith and live with enthusiasm the commitments of the Militia of Mary Immaculate, to which you belong, following the teaching and examples of Fr. Maximiliam Kolbe. "To suffer, work, love and rejoice": this was his program and the summary of his life. May it be also for you, with the help of the Blessed Virgin. And my blessing, which I impart with great affection to you and to all the members of your Militia, always accompany you.

October 10, 1982
Canonization Homily
Pope John Paul II, Rome

"**G**REATER LOVE HAS NO MAN THAN THIS, THAT A MAN lay down his life for his friends" (Jn 15:13). From today the Church wishes to give the title of saint to a man who was enabled to carry out absolutely literally the above words of the redeemer.

For toward the end of July 1941, when the camp commandant ordered the prisoners destined to die of starvation to be lined up, this man, Maximilian Maria Kolbe, offered himself spontaneously and said that he was ready to go to death in the place of one of them. This readiness was accepted, and after more than two weeks of torment caused by starvation, Father Maximilian's life was ended with a lethal injection, August 14, 1941.

All this happened in the concentration camp at Auschwitz where, during the last war, some four million people were put to death, including also the servant of God Edith Stein (the Carmelite Sister Teresa Benedicta of the Cross), whose beatification cause is at present under examination at the competent

143

congregation. Disobedience to God—the creator of life, who has said "Thou shalt not kill"—caused in that place the immense holocaust of so many innocent people. And so at the same time, our age was thus horribly marked by the murder of the innocent man.

2) Father Maximilian Kolbe, himself being a prisoner of the concentration camp, defended in that place of death the right to life of an innocent man, one of the four million. This man (Franciszek Gajowniczek) is still living and is here among us. Father Kolbe defended his right to life, declaring that he was ready to go to death in his place because he was the father of a family and his life was necessary to his dear ones. Father Maximilian Maria Kolbe thus reaffirmed the creator's exclusive right to the life of an innocent man and bore witness to Christ and to love. For the apostle John writes: "By this we know love, that he laid down his life for us; and we ought to lay down our lives for the brethren" (1 Jn 3:16).

By laying down his life for a brother, Father Maximilian, whom the Church has since 1971 venerated as "blessed," in a particular way made himself like Christ.

3) We, therefore, who today October 10 are gathered before the Basilica of St. Peter in Rome, wish to express the special value of which the death by martyrdom of Father Maximilian Kolbe has in the eyes of God:

"Precious in the sight of the Lord is the death of his saints" (Ps 115 (116):15). These are the words we have repeated in the responsorial psalm. It is truly precious and inestimable. Through the death which Christ underwent on the cross, the redemption of the world was achieved, for this death has the value of supreme love. Through the death undergone by Father Maximilian Kolbe a shining sign of this love was renewed in our century, which is so seriously and in so many ways threatened by sin and death.

144

In this canonization liturgy there seems to appear before us that "martyr of love" of Oswiecim (as Paul VI called him), saying "O Lord, I am thy servant; I am thy servant, the son of thy handmaid. Thou hast loosed my bonds" (Ps 115 (116):16).

And, as though gathering together the sacrifice of his whole life, he, a priest and a spiritual son of St. Francis, seems to say:

"What shall I render to the Lord for all his bounty to me?"

"I will lift up the cup of salvation and call on the name of the Lord" (Ps 115 (116):12f).

These are words of gratitude. Death undergone out of love, in the place of one's brother, is a heroic act of man through which, together with the *beatus*, we glorify God. For from God comes the grace of such heroism, of this martyrdom.

4) Therefore let us glorify today God's great work in man. Before all of us gathered here Father Maximilian Kolbe lifts up his "cup of salvation," in which is contained the sacrifice of his whole life, sealed with the martyr's death "for a brother."

Maximilian prepared for this definitive sacrifice by following Christ from the first years of his life in Poland. From those years comes the mysterious dream of two crowns: one white and one red, among which our saint does not choose, but accepts them both. From the years of his youth, in fact, he was filled with a great love of Christ and the desire for martyrdom.

This love and this desire accompanied him along the path of his Franciscan and priestly vocation, for which he prepared himself both in Poland and in Rome. This love and this desire followed him through all the places of his priestly and Franciscan service in Poland, and also of his missionary service in Japan.

5) The inspiration of his whole life was the Immaculate Virgin, to whom he entrusted his love for Christ and his desire for martyrdom. In the mystery of the Immaculate Conception there revealed itself before the eyes of his soul that marvelous and

145

supernatural world of God's grace offered to man. The faith and works of the whole life of Father Maximilian show that he thought of his cooperation with divine grace as a soldierly service under the banner of the Immaculate Conception. The Marian characteristic is particularly expressive in the life and holiness of Father Kolbe. His whole apostolate, both in his homeland and on the missions, was similarly marked with this sign. Both in Poland and in Japan the centers of this apostolate were the special Cities of the Immaculate (*Niepokalanow* in Poland, *Mugenzai No Sono* in Japan).

6) What happened in the starvation bunker in the concentration camp of Oswiecim (Auschwitz) August 14, 1941?

The reply is given by today's liturgy: "God tested" Maximilian Maria "and found him worthy of himself" (cf. Wis 3:5). God tested him "like gold in the furnace and like a sacrificial burnt offering he accepted him" (cf. Wis 3:6).

Even if "in the sight of men he was punished," yet "his hope is full of immortality," for "the souls of the righteous are in the hand of God, and no torment will ever touch them." And when, humanly speaking, torment and death come to them, when "in the eyes of men they seemed to have died," when "their departure from us was thought to be an affliction . . .they are at peace." They experience life and glory "in the hands of God" (cf. Wis 3:1-4).

This life is the fruit of death like Christ's death. Glory is the sharing of his resurrection. So what happened in the starvation bunker, August 14, 1941?

There were fulfilled the words spoken by Christ to the apostles in order that they "should go and bear fruit and that their fruit should abide" (cf. Jn 15:16).

In a marvelous way the fruit of the heroic death of Maximilian Kolbe endures in the Church and the world.

7) Men saw what happened in the camp at Auschwitz. And even if to their eyes it must have seemed that a companion of their torment "died," even if humanly speaking they could consider "his departure" as "a disaster," nevertheless in their minds this was not simply "death."

Maximilian did not die, but "gave his life . . . for his brother."

In that death, terrible from the human point of view, there was the whole definitive greatness of the human act and of the human choice: he spontaneously offered himself up to death out of love.

An in this human death of his there was the clear witness borne to Christ: the witness borne to Christ to the dignity of man, to the sanctity of his life and to the saving power of death, in which the power of love is made manifest.

Precisely for this reason the death of Maximilian Kolbe became a sign of victory. This was victory won over all the systems of contempt and hate for man and for what is divine in man, a victory like that won by our Lord Jesus Christ on Calvary.

"You are my friends if you do what I command you" (Jn 15:14).

8) The Church accepts this sign of victory, won through the power of Christ's redemption, with reverence and gratitude. She seeks to discern its eloquence with all humility and love.

As ever when the Church proclaims the holiness of her sons and daughters, as also in the present case, she seeks to act with all due exactness and responsibility, searching into all the aspects of the life and death of the Servant of God.

Yet at the same time the Church must be careful as she reads the sign of holiness given by God in his earthly servant not to allow its full eloquence and definitive meaning to go unnoticed.

And so, in judging the cause of Blessed Maximilian Kolbe— even after his beatification—it was necessary to take into consideration many voices of the people of God and especially of our brothers in the episcopate, both in Poland and also in Germany, who asked that Maximilian Kolbe be proclaimed as a martyr saint.

Before the eloquence of the life and death of Blessed Maximilian, it is impossible not to recognize what seems to constitute the man and essential element of the sign given by God to the Church and the world in his death.

Does not this death, faced spontaneously for love of man, constitute a particular fulfillment of the words of Christ?

Does not his death make Maximilian particularly like to Christ, the model of all martyrs, who gives his own life on the cross for his brothers?

Does not such a death possess a particular and penetrating eloquence for our age?

Does not this death constitute a particularly authentic witness of the Church in the modern world?

9) And so, in virtue of my apostolic authority I have decreed that Maximilian Maria Kolbe, who after his beatification was venerated as a confessor, shall henceforward be venerated also as a martyr.

"Precious in the eyes of the Lord is the death of his faithful ones." Amen.

December 8, 1982
Homily at St. Mary Major
Pope John Paul II, Rome

"HAIL, FULL OF GRACE, THE LORD IS WITH YOU" (LK 1:28). While these words of the angel's greeting softly re-echo in our mind, I wish to turn my glance, along with you, dear brothers and sisters, to the mystery of the Immaculate Conception of the Blessed Virgin Mary, with *the spiritual eye of Saint Maximilian Kolbe*. He bound all the works of his life and his vocation to Mary Immaculate. And therefore this year, in which he was elevated to the glory of the saints, he has much to tell us on the solemnity of Mary Immaculate, whose devout "militant" he loved to call himself.

His love for Mary Immaculate was indeed the center of his spiritual life, the fruitful inspiring principle of his apostolic activity. The sublime model of Mary Immaculate illuminated and guided his entire existence along his ways in the world and made his heroic death in the extermination camp of *Auschwitz* a splendid Christian and priestly witness. With the

149

intuition of a saint and the refinement of a theologian, Maximilian Kolbe meditated with extraordinary insight on the mystery of Mary's Immaculate Conception in the light of Sacred Scripture, the Magisterium, and the Liturgy of the Church, drawing from them wonderful lessons for life. He has appeared in our time as a prophet and an apostle of a new "Marian era," destined to make Jesus Christ and his Gospel shine with a bright light in the entire world.

This mission that he carried out with ardour and dedication, "classified him," as Paul VI stated in the homily at his beatification, "among the great saints and clairvoyant minds that have understood, venerated and sung the mystery of Mary" (*Insegnamenti di Paolo VI*, IX, 1971, p. 909). Though he was aware of the inexhaustible depths of the mystery of the Immaculate Conception, for which "human words are not able to describe her who became the Mother of God" (Writings of Maximilian Kolbe, *Hero of Oswiecim and Blessed of the Church*, Vol. 3, Ed. Città di Vita, Florence, 1975, v. III, p. 690), his greatest regret was that Mary Immaculate was not sufficiently known and loved after the example of Jesus Christ and how the Tradition of the Church and the examples of the saints teach us. Indeed, in loving Mary we honor God, who raised her to the dignity of the Mother of his Son made man, and we unite ourselves with Jesus Christ who loved her as a mother. We will never love her as he loved her: "Jesus was the first to honor her as his mother, and we must imitate him in this also. We will never be able to equal the love with which Jesus loved her" (*ibid.*, v. II, p. 351). Love for Mary, Father Maximilian states, is the simplest and easiest way to sanctify ourselves, fulfilling our Christian vocation. The love of which he speaks is certainly not a superficial sentimentalism, but it is a generous commitment, it is a giving of the whole person, as he himself showed us with his life of evangelical fidelity right up to his heroic death.

2) St. Maximilian Kolbe's attention was incessantly concentrated on Mary's Immaculate Conception in order to be able to gather the marvelous wealth contained in the name that she herself revealed and that constitutes the explanation of what today's Gospel teaches us in the words of the Angel Gabriel: "Hail, full of grace, the Lord is with you" (Lk 1:28). Recalling the apparitions at Lourdes—which for him were a stimulus and an incentive to better understand the fonts of Revelation—he observes: "To Saint Bernadette, who had questioned her many times, the Virgin answered, 'I am the Immaculate Conception.' With these words she clearly revealed that she not only is conceived without sin, but she is moreover the very 'Immaculate Conception,' just as a white object is one thing and whiteness is something else; a perfect thing is one thing, perfection is something else" (*ibid.*, v. III, p. 516). The Immaculate Conception is the name which reveals with precision who Mary is: it not only affirms a quality, but it exactly defines her person: Mary is radically holy in the totality of her existence, from the very beginning.

3) The sublime, supernatural grandeur was granted to Mary with regard to Jesus Christ; it is in him and through him that God shared with her the fullness of sanctity. Mary is Immaculate because she is the Mother of God, and she became the Mother of God because she is Immaculate, Maximilian Kolbe states in clear-cut terms. Mary's Immaculate Conception manifests in a unique and sublime way the absolute centrality and the universal salvific role of Jesus Christ. "From the divine motherhood flow all the graces given to the Most Holy Virgin Mary, and the first of these is her Immaculate Conception" (*ibid.*, v. III, p. 475). For this reason Mary is not simply like Eve before original sin, but she was enriched with a fullness of incomparable grace because she is the Mother of Christ, and the Immaculate Conception was the beginning of a prodigious uninterrupted growth of her supernatural life.

4) The mystery of Mary's sanctity must be contemplated in the totality of the divine order of salvation in order to be grasped in a harmonious way, lest it appear that this privilege seperates her from the Church, which is the Body of Christ. Father Maximilian takes great pains to tie Mary's Immaculate Conception and her role in the plan of salvation to the mystery of the Trinity, and in a completely special way to the Person of the Holy Spirit. With profound cleverness he developed the multiple aspects contained in the notion of "Spouse of the Holy Spirit," well known in patristic and theological tradition and suggested by the New Testament: "The Holy Spirit will come upon you and the power of the Most High will overshadow you; hence the holy offspring to be born will be called Son of God" (Lk 1:35). It is an analogy, Saint Maximilian Kolbe stresses, that gives a glimpse of the ineffable, intimate and fruitful union between the Holy Spirit and Mary. "The Holy Spirit established his dwelling in Mary from the very first moment of her existence, he took absolute possession of her and so pervaded her that the name of Spouse of the Holy Spirit cannot express more than a far-off, pale, imperfect shadow of this union" (*ibid.*, v. III, p. 515).

5) Investigating with ecstatic admiration the divine plan of salvation, which has its source in the Father who willed to communicate freely to creatures the divine life of Jesus Christ, and which was manifested in Mary Immaculate in a marvelous way, Father Kolbe, fascinated and enraptured, exclaims, "There is love everywhere" (*ibid.*, v. III, p. 690). The gratuitous love of God is the answer to all questions. "God is love," St. John affirms (1 Jn 4:8). Everything that exists is a reflection of the free love of God, and therefore every creature expresses in some way its infinite splendour. In a particular way, love is the center and vertex of the human person, made in the image and likeness of God. Mary Immaculate, the highest and most perfect of human persons, eminently reproduces the image of God and is therefore made capable of loving him with incomparable intensity as the Immaculate, without distractions or slackening. She is the unique handmaid of the Lord (cf. Lk 1:38) who with her free and personal *fiat* responds to God's love by always doing what he asks of her. As the response of every other creature, hers is not an autonomous response, but it is a grace and a gift of God. In this response there is involved all of her freedom, the freedom of the Immaculate. "In the union of the Holy Spirit with Mary, love does not join only these two persons, but the first love is all the love of the Most Holy Trinity, while the second, Mary's, is all the love of creation, and so in this union heaven is united to earth, all the uncreated Love with all created love. . . . It is the vertex of love" (*ibid.*, v. III, p. 758).

The circulating nature of love, which originates from the Father and which in Mary's response returns to its source, is a characteristic and fundamental aspect of Father Kolbe's Marian thought. It is this principle that is at the base of his Christian anthropology, his view of the history and the spiritual life of every person. Mary Immaculate is the archetype and fullness of every creature love; her crystal-clear and most intense love for God includes in its perfection that fragile and soiled love of other creatures. Mary's response is that of all humanity.

All this does not obscure nor diminish the absolute centrality of Jesus Christ in the order of salvation, but illuminates it and proclaims it vigorously, because Mary derives all her grandeur from him. As the history of the Church teaches, Mary's role is to make her Son shine, to lead to him, and to help welcome him.

The continual theological investigation of the mystery of Mary Immaculate became for Maximilian Kolbe the source and the motive for unlimited giving and extraordinary dynamism. He truly knew how to incorporate the truth into life, also because he attained a knowledge of Mary, as all the saints, not only from reflection guided by faith, but especially from prayer. "Anyone who is not capable of bending his knees and imploring from Mary in humble prayer the grace to know who she really is, cannot hope to learn more about her" (*ibid.*, v. III, p.474).

6) And now, receiving this final exhortation of the heroic son of Poland and the authentic messenger of Marian devotion, gathered in this splendid basilica for the Eucharistic Prayer in honor of the Immaculate Conception, we will bend our knees before her image and will repeat to her, with that ardour and filial piety that so distinguished Saint Maximilian, the words of the angel: "Hail, full of grace, the Lord is with you." Amen.

February 26, 1994
Address celebrating the 100th anniversary of St. Maximilian's birth
Pope John Paul II to
Conventual Franciscan Student-friars, Rome

DEAR YOUNG CONFRERES OF ST. MAXIMILIAN KOLBE, I AF-
fectionately welcome you today and I extend my cor-
dial greeting to you. My greeting goes especially to
the Minister General of the Friars Minor Conventual, Fr.
Lanfranco Serrini, whom I thank for the kind words with which
he just addressed me, also on behalf of the authorities of the
Militia of the Immaculata, of your teachers and of each one of
you. You are gathered here to commemorate the first centenary of the birth of St. Maximilian Kolbe, martyr of love and
patron of our difficult century. This anniversary is an occasion
for prayer, reflection and renewed effort, especially on this great
eve of the year 2000.

Fr. Maximilian Maria Kolbe, born January 8, 1894, in
Zdunska Wola, Poland, was a shining figure because of the
strong love with which he consecrated his life to the Immacu-

late Virgin and because of the heroic gift of his life for his brothers, that sacrifice which led him to his terrible death in the bunker of Auschwitz. He remains with us as a *prophet and a sign of the new era, the era of the civilization of love.*

Even as a cleric at the Seraphicum College here in Rome, he tried to share with his fellow students the radical nature of consecration to the Immaculate Virgin, urging them to be soldiers of her who was given to us as the dawn which precedes the rising Sun that saves, Christ the Lord. Thus he wrote that he wanted to entrust them with the task of "radiating the Immaculata in our environment, attracting other souls to her, so that even the hearts of our neighbors would be opened before her and she could reign in the hearts of everyone, and everywhere, without distinction of race, nationality or language, as also in the hearts of all people who will live in every age, until the end of time" (SK 1210, III, 475). Throughout the world, many followed him, with the audacity of hope, in loyalty to their vocations, in the austerity of their lives, aware that— as he loved to repeat—"*only love creates.*" But the optimism with which Father Kolbe faced his everyday life never caused him to forget that it is in life that *the constant struggle between grace and sin, between loyalty and disloyalty, takes place* (cf. Rom 7:14-25). And it was precisely when evil seemed to have prevailed over him, in the horror of the extermination camp, that Christ's victory fully appeared.

"Only love creates." Sin destroys.

Fr. Maximilian Kolbe *reaffirmed*, by his brave witness, *the power of the new creation*, of which Mary Immaculate is the anticipation and the example by virtue of being the predestined Mother of the Redeemer.

Our century has known many martyrs who gave their lives to confirm their faith in the God of life. One of the Church's tasks today is certainly to *preserve the memory of these men and women, our brothers and sisters, who taught us how to open our lives to Christ in order to proclaim him to everyone* (cf. Col 1:23), in every corner of the earth, as your confrere, Father Kolbe, did. From their blood a new youthfulness arose in the Church: humanity today needs this springtime of hope. When man wants to create a civilization that excludes God from his horizon, he commits horrendous crimes and causes terrible disasters. Every time that men have tried to build their cities without values deriving from "belonging to God" (cf. 1 Jn 4:6), they have ended up building walls and barriers between one another.

Dear young people, you are entrusted with the ever timely message which St. Maximilian confirmed by his supreme sacrifice. "Every generation," he observed, "must add its own labor and its own fruit to those of the preceding generations . . . . What can we contribute? The second page of our history is beginning now: to bring the Immaculata into men's hearts so that she may erect the throne of her Son in them, lead them to knowledge of him and enflame them with love for the Sacred heart of Jesus" (SK 486 I, 894-895).

It is a full program that involves one's whole life. It is entrusted to your energies and your commitment. Love the Immaculata, since it is she who leads you to the Son. Through her and with her help, you will be able to overcome the inevitable difficulties you will find along your way. With her, you will be given the seed of *Christ, the center and goal of every life*, that you may plant it in the heart of every person you meet. Call upon her then with trust and tenderness, so that you too may, like St. Maximilian, be true witnesses to the love of God for every person.

In cordially offering you the greeting of "Peace and all Good," which is so dear to you, I gladly bless you all.

SELECTED MARIOLOGICAL WRITINGS OF ST. MAXIMILIAN

Selections from Father Kolbe's Conferences

June 23, 1936
The Mediation of the Immaculata

JESUS THE MAN-GOD CAME TO US NOT ONLY AS OUR SAVIOR, but also as the Mediator of perfect adoration towards God. The glory which man could give to God was limited and imperfect, because it came from a creature, whereas God is infinite and hence deserves infinite adoration.

Since Jesus came to us, we terminate all our prayers "through Jesus Christ, our Lord." Through Christ we can now pay homage to God the Father. The glory which we give to Christ is transformed by him into infinite praise for the Father. Such homage is thenceforth perfect, because it is offered to God by Christ. Still, we know by our experience how weak we are, how full of defects in our daily living. Therefore, this glory given to Christ is stained by sin, and imperfect.

How far we remain from the kind of adoration that divine justice deserves!

Except for our most holy Mother, all human beings give Jesus imperfect glory. So, because of this wretchedness of ours, we need an intermediary. Just as God the Father gives us Jesus Christ as our Mediator, so too does Christ give us the Immaculata to be our Mediatrix. She never knew the slightest sin; she is indeed the only creature who gives God truly unsullied glory; and Jesus offers his Father infinite homage. Thus, the glory which we render to Jesus through the Immaculata is truly unspoiled and infinite, worthy of God's own greatness.

June 27, 1936
Mary, the "Bridge" to the Trinitarian Life

The life of the Blessed Trinity had no beginning, and will have no end. It is immutable. From all eternity the Father begets the Son, and from all eternity the Holy Spirit proceeds from Father and Son. The Father acts through the Son, and the Son through the Holy Spirit. This is something we cannot really understand with our limited intelligence; the least attempt to explain it leaves us bewildered. Such then is the inner life of the Trinity: the Father acts through the Son and the Son through the Holy Spirit. This life of God is reflected in varying degrees in God's creatures. It has repercussions throughout the universe as though in a series of echoes, faint and remote. . . .

Among all creatures, man is the most exalted; and among all human beings the Immaculata is the sublimest. She is God's most perfect creature, free from the slightest taint of sin, Immaculate.

Everywhere in nature and in the laws that govern it, we find the phenomenon of action and reaction. This is a reflection of the life of the Trinity. God is action; he creates everything out of nothing; creatures are the reaction; more or less perfectly they tend towards and return to their Creator.

There are, then, three divine Persons: the Father, the Son, and the Holy Spirit. The Father acts through the Son, and the Son through the Holy Spirit; and, like a bridge between the Holy Spirit and the rest of creation we find the most perfect creature of all, the Immaculata. Among the Father, Son and

Holy Spirit there exists a single and unique activity, the activity of the three divine Persons, the perfection of which can in no way be limited. On the other hand, our relations with God, with the Holy Spirit, are far from perfect. This is why we need a bridge; and this bridge is the Immaculata.

Everything that the Holy Spirit receives from the Son, and that the Son receives from the Father, the Holy Spirit gives to the Immaculata; by her he acts in other creatures. This is why the Immaculata is called the Spouse of the Holy Spirit. This too is something our mere human intellect cannot really understand, it is so far above us.

Jesus Christ has two natures, divine and human, united in one divine Person, the Word. The Immaculata is so closely united with the Holy Spirit that we cannot understand their union. Still we can at least say that the Holy Spirit and the Immaculata are two persons living in such intimate union that they share one sole life. Hence all the graces which come from the Father by the Son and the Holy Spirit come to us through the Mother of God; for this reason she is our Mediatrix.

Even if we don't think about it, or when we pray to the Lord Jesus or the saints, all the graces we receive come to us through Mary alone. If we are unwilling to receive them from her we shall get none; and in so acting we are upsetting the order established by God's will. This is one reason why Satan tries by all the means in his power to get us to break away from whatever binds us to the Immaculata.

February 11, 1938
Lourdes: "Confirmation of the Entire Catholic Faith"
Ever since Original Sin was committed, human intelligence has remained darkened so that it cannot rise to the knowledge of the causes of everything. Our first parents in Eden understood everything very well; their intelligence was clear and lively; but after they sinned, all that was changed. For this reason,

when God wishes to make himself known to men he gives them signs and works miracles. We find many miracles in the Old Testament, and even more in the New. When Jesus was in this world he said: "Even if you do not believe in me, believe in my works" (Jn 10:38).

The miracle of the Resurrection is the foundation of our faith. The disciples of Jesus were weak; even though they had seen many miracles, at the time of his arrest they all abandoned him. Only when Jesus had risen was their faith confirmed, and were they given the courage to endure suffering and persecution.

Since Christ's resurrection, from time to time miracles happen, to reinforce our faith; such were the apparitions at Lourdes . . . . There the Immaculata chose a weak instrument to manifest her power. There were many objections; people said, "It isn't true." But all the while the miraculous fountain was flowing, and many miracles and conversions took place. What did the Most Blessed Virgin then do, after establishing her credibility by these miracles? In public before the whole crowd of people she said who she was, confirming the dogma of the Immaculate Conception which had been defined in 1854. She said of herself, "I am the Immaculate Conception." If she is indeed the Immaculate Conception, then everything which serves as a foundation for this truth is also true. Hence the apparitions at Lourdes are a confirmation of the entire Catholic faith. This is why these apparitions of the Most Blessed Virgin at Lourdes are so important.

July 26, 1939
Who is the Immaculata?

Who is Mary Immaculate?

To this abrupt question it is not possible to give a satisfactory answer, because this mystery transcends our human intelligence.

In the Litany of Loreto we find many beautiful titles attributed to the Mother of God; but beautiful as they are, they are not enough. Scripture says little about her; it merely relates a few facts, like the Annunciation, the Nativity, and so on. St. John would have been able to tell us a lot more no doubt, since he was, for so many years, the witness of Mary's blessed life.

One would have to set down all the various graces bestowed throughout the history of nations, to tell of the many apparitions . . . but especially one would have to recount the story of grace in each individual soul, if one wished to give even a partial answer to the question, "Who is the Immaculata?"

She is the Mother of God, and her name is the Immaculata. When God showed himself to Moses he said of himself, "I am the One who is" (Ex 3:14); in other words, "I am BEING itself."

When St. Bernadette asked the Most Blessed Mother her name, Mary replied: "I am the Immaculate Conception." Such is the Immaculata defined by her own words.

But what does the expression "Immaculate Conception" mean?

The word "conception" tells us that she is not eternal; that she had a beginning. "Immaculate" tells us that from the first instant of her existence there never was in her the least conflict with God's will. The Immaculata is the most perfect of all creatures; she is the most sublime; she is divine.

She was immaculate because she was to become the Mother of God; she became the Mother of God because she was immaculate.

Mother of God!

The human mind cannot grasp what God is; neither can we comprehend the dignity of the Mother of God. It is easier to understand a title like "servant of God"; "daughter of God" is more difficult to grasp; but "Mother of God" transcends our minds completely.

God calls creatures into being when he creates them. Then, in their movement of return to God these creatures draw near to him and come to resemble their Creator more and more.

God comes to his most perfect creature, the Immaculata; and the fruit of their love is Jesus Christ, the Mediator between the Creator and all creatures.

When we ask, "Who is the Immaculata?" our language is not able to furnish an adequate response. We can't even form a meaningful idea of it. . . .

True knowledge of the Immaculata can only be acquired in prayer. The purer a soul is, the greater efforts it makes to avoid sin—and if it does happen to sin, it tries its best to rise from sin and to make up for its fault by love—the more humble it is, and the more spirit of penance it shows, the more and better will it get to know the Immaculata.

Miles Immaculatae, 1938
Why Mary is Our Mediatrix

THE STRICT UNION THAT EXISTS AMONG THE TRUTHS OF
Christian doctrine is known to us all. For Catholic
dogmas are born from one another and perfect each
other reciprocally. We can see an example of this in the Fathers
of the Council of Ephesus. They proclaimed the divine Motherhood of Mary solely on the basis of the Catholic doctrine
regarding the hypostatic union of the divine and human natures in the Person of the Word.

Once the relationship between Jesus and his Mother Mary
became known, there arose the Catholic belief which holds
that the Mother of the Savior was exempt from original sin.
Catholics did not dare think that Mary had ever been enslaved
to the devil even for a single instant. A wonderful hope of ob-
taining the sweet care of Mary also arose among the faithful
based on the preeminent mission of the Blessed Virgin and on
her unutterable union (her Immaculate Conception) with the
Holy Spirit.

Immaculate Conception Linked to Mediation

And it is now clear that our relationship to Mary the Co-Redemptrix and Dispenser of graces in the economy of the redemption has not been understood from the beginning with uniform clarity. Nevertheless our belief in the mediation of the Blessed Virgin Mary is daily growing greater. In this brief article we want to show what the dogma of the Immaculate Conception of the Blessed Virgin Mary contributes to the doctrine of Mary's mediation.

The work of our redemption depends directly on the Second Person of God, Jesus Christ. By his blood He reconciled us to the Father, for with it he made satisfaction for the sin of Adam and merited for us sanctifying grace, various actual graces and the right to enter heaven.

Still, the Third Person of the Most Holy Trinity also participates in this work in that He transforms the souls of men into temples of God by the power of the redemption achieved by Christ, and He makes us children of God by adoption and heirs of the kingdom of heaven, according to the words of St. Paul:

> You have been washed, you have been justified in the name of our Lord Jesus Christ and in the Spirit of our God. (1 Cor 6:11)

The Holy Spirit, who is God-Love, unites us to the other two divine Persons when He descends into our souls. For this reason St. Paul writes in his letter to the Romans:

> We do not know what to pray for as we should, but the Holy Spirit Himself pleads for us with un-speakable groanings. (Rom 8:26)

In the epistle to the Corinthians he also says the distribution of graces depends on the will of the Holy Spirit:

> To one indeed is given the speaking of wisdom through the Spirit, to another the speaking of knowledge . . . to another the gift of healing in the same Spirit; to another the

working of wonders, to another prophecy . . . One and the same Spirit however does all these things. (1 Cor 12:8-11).

Immaculate Heart Is Sign of Holy Spirit

Still, just as Jesus became the God-Man in order to reveal his immense love for us, so also the Third Divine Person, God-Love, willed to show his mediation with the Father and the Son in some external image. That this image is the Immaculate Heart of the Virgin is clear from the words of the saints, especially those who hold Mary is the Spouse of the Holy Spirit. Whence Bl. Louis Marie Grignion draws the conclusion according to the mind of the Fathers:

> The Holy Spirit lacks fruitfulness in God, that is, no divine Person proceeds from him. But he becomes fruitful through Mary whom he has taken to himself as Spouse. With her and in her and through her he produces his most illustrious work, the incarnation of the Word: "The Holy Spirit will come upon you, and the power of the Most High will overshadow you" (Lk 1:35). Still, this is not to be understood in the sense that the Blessed Virgin has brought fruitfulness to the Holy Spirit. As God he would already have had this fruitfulness just as have the Father and the Son, even though he had not revealed it by action in that no Divine Person proceeds from him. Rather it is to be understood in the sense that the Holy Spirit has chosen to manifest his fruitfulness by the mediation of Mary, which certainly he does not absolutely need, by producing the human nature of Christ through her and with her.

Even after the death of Christ the Holy Spirit accomplishes everything in us through Mary. For the words of the Creator pronounced to the serpent concerning the Immaculata: "She shall crush your head" (Gen 3:15) are, according to the teaching of the theologians, to be understood without limitation in regard to time.

167

The work of forming the new members of the predestined of the Mystical Body of Christ belongs to the Holy Spirit. But as Bl. Louis Grignion demonstrates, this work is done with Mary, in Mary and through Mary.

Holy Spirit and Mary Enable Us to Know Christ

We are led to this conclusion, namely that the Holy Spirit acts through Mary, by the texts of Sacred Scripture and the words of the saints, who are the best interpreters of Sacred Scripture: "And I will ask the Father, and he will give you another Paraclete, so that he might abide with you for eternity, the Spirit of truth . . . (Jn 14:16-17). The Paraclete, the Holy Spirit, however, which the Father will send in my name, he is the one who will teach you all things and bring to your minds all that I have said to you . . . (Jn 14:26); however when the Spirit of truth shall have come, he will teach you all the truth . . . . He will glorify me . . ." (Jn 6:13-14).

Bl. Louis Grignion uses words of almost the same meaning in regard to the Immaculata:

> We have not yet known Mary, and for this reason we also do not know Christ as we should. If however Christ is to become known and his kingdom is to come upon the earth—which has to come to pass regardless this will result solely from Mary's being known, and from her reign over us; for Mary gave birth to Jesus for the salvation of the world in the first place, and now renders us fit to know him clearly.

Therefore, just as the Second Person of God appears in the flesh bearing the name "seed of the woman," so also the Holy Spirit reveals his share in the work of redemption through the Immaculate Virgin whom he has conjoined with himself most profoundly in a manner surpassing all our power to understand, but preserving into the Personhood of each of them. Their union, therefore, is different from the hypostatic union

168

that unites the two natures, divine and human, in the one sole Person of Christ; nevertheless, this difference in no way prevents the action of Mary from being the most perfect action of the Holy Spirit. For Mary, as the Spouse of the Holy Spirit and who is, therefore, raised above all created perfection, fulfills in every way the will of the Holy Spirit who dwells in her and with her and this from the first instant of her conception.

Mediation Based on "Marriage" with the Holy Spirit

From all that has been presented here we can rightly conclude that Mary as the Mother of the Savior Jesus has been made the Co-Redemptrix of the human race, and that as the Spouse of the Holy Spirit she participates in the distribution of all the graces. Whence we can say with the theologians: ". . . as the first Eve worked for our downfall by her truly personal and free actions, and truly helped cause it, so Mary by her truly personal actions joined in the reparation . . . in this there is already in a most evident way true mediation properly speaking."[1]

In recent times especially we are perceiving the Immaculata, the Spouse of the Holy Spirit, as our Mediatrix.

It was in the year 1830 that the Immaculate Virgin appeared to Sister Catherine Labouré. We learn from the account of this novice that the purpose of the apparition of Mary was to reveal her Immaculate Conception and her astonishing power with God:

> The most holy Virgin cast her eyes on me and at the same time I heard a voice say, "This globe of the world represents all men and each individual person." And again: "Behold the symbol of the graces which I pour out on all who invoke me."
>
> Afterwards an oval figure was formed around the most holy Virgin in which the following invocation was written in golden words: "O Mary conceived without sin, pray for us who have recourse to you." At the same moment I heard

a voice saying: "Strike a medal according to this exemplar: all who carry it will overflow with graces."

Mary Acts as Mediatrix at Lourdes

At Lourdes the Immaculate Virgin prodded all men to do penance; finally she recited the "Hail Mary" in order to show it to us as a source of help. From that moment the Immaculata at Lourdes began to act in her capacity as our Mediatrix: she invites the sick to come, she gathers the weak and the lame to cure them, and she reveals our dependence on her even in natural life.

The sick in soul, namely unbelievers and sinners with hardened hearts she draws sweetly and pours supernatural life into their hearts in order to convince them of her power to grant us supernatural life.

Moreover, we should note this above all, that Jesus works miracles in the place (Lourdes) chosen by his Mother.

Everything that the Blessed Virgin Mary does at Lourdes testifies to the truth of the words of St. Peter Damian: "A curse came upon the earth through a woman; through a woman earth's blessing is restored."[2] And also the words of St. Augustine: "In man's deception, poison was served him through a woman; in his redemption, salvation is presented him through a woman."[3]

Therefore what St. Bernard expresses in words, the Immaculate Virgin confirms by acts: "Such is the desire of him who willed that we should have everything through Mary."[4]

Father Maximilian

---

[1] J. Bittremieux De Mediatione universale B.V.M.

[2] "Homilia in Nativitate Virginis" PL 144, 758.

[3] "Sermo" 51, c. 2. PL 38, 335.

[4] Quoted in St. Alphonsus Ligouri in *The Glories of Mary*.

1940
Father Kolbe's Sketches for a Book

We Must Be Intimately United to the Immaculata

Immaculata, Virgin Mother, to thee I turn in humble prayer: "Grant that I may praise thee, O holy Virgin; give me strength against thine enemies!" (Duns Scotus).

How true it is that human language is incapable of expressing heavenly realities! How can we understand and express what God has done in thee and through thee?

Then the Immaculata appears in this world, without the least stain of sin, the masterpiece of God's hands, full of grace. God, the Most Holy Trinity, beholds the lowliness (i.e. the humility, the root of all her other virtues) of his handmaid, and "does great things for her, he the Almighty" (cf. Lk 1:49). God the Father gives her his own Son to be her Son; God the Son descends into her womb; and God the Holy Spirit forms the body of Christ in the womb of this most pure virgin. "And the Word was made flesh" (Jn 1:14). The Immaculata becomes the Mother of God. The fruit of the love of God in his trinitarian life and of Mary the Immaculata, is Christ, the God-Man.

Henceforth all the other sons of God must be modeled after this first Son of God, the Man-God, the infinite One. They must reproduce his traits; by imitating Christ souls reach sanctity. The more sedulously one tries to reflect in himself the image of Christ, the nearer will he approach God, the more fully will he share in the divinity, the more truly will he be a man-God. This is the union brought about by the spousal love of the soul for Christ, through its resemblance to him, and by God's action.

But if anyone does not wish to have Mary Immaculate for his Mother, he will not have Christ for his Brother; the Father will not send the Son to him; the Son will not come down into his soul; the Holy Spirit will not make him a member of the mystical body through the gift of his grace; because all God's marvels of grace take place in Mary Immaculate who is full of grace—and in her alone. For no other creature is or ever will be immaculate, or full of grace, the Lord will not be with anyone unless he is intimately united with the Immaculate Virgin. And since the First-born Son, the God-man, was conceived only with the specific consent of the Most Blessed Virgin, the same must hold true for all men, who must be conformed to their first Model in all things.

The Meaning of the Name "Immaculate Conception"

"Immaculate Conception" does not mean, as some have thought, that the most Blessed Virgin had no earthly father. Like all other children of our race she was born in a true family; she had a true father and a true mother. She was "conceived," hence she is not God who has neither beginning nor end; nor is she an angel created directly by God; nor is she like our first parents who did not come into being through conception.

Further, she calls herself the "conception," not after the fashion of Jesus who, even though he was conceived, exists as God from all eternity.

But she says, "Immaculate Conception." This is what sets her apart from all other children of the human race.

Thus, the name "Immaculate Conception" belongs to her, and to her alone.

The Immaculata's Union with the Trinity

Our Father in Heaven is the first Principle and the last End of all things.

Human intelligence and human language, although so handicapped, have tried to think about God and to speak of him. What we can understand about God is not really adequate, yet it is true as far as it goes.

Through divine revelation we know that from all eternity the Father begets the Son and the Holy Spirit proceeds from Father and Son. This life of the most Holy Trinity is re-echoed in numberless and various ways by the creatures that issue from God's hands. God is One in the Holy Trinity, his creatures are like him in more or less remote ways. The universal principle according to which every effect resembles its cause applies here all the more fully and exactly in so far as God creates everything from nothing; thus there is nothing in creation which is not God's work.

Every act of love in God comes forth from the Father through the Son and the Holy Spirit. God creates, maintains in existence, gives life and growth in the natural as well as in the supernatural order. In his love God supports in existence all his innumerable limited created resemblances; and the love-reaction that is provoked in the creature can return to the Father only through the Holy Spirit and the Son. . . . We may not always realize this fully, yet such is the case. No one but God is the author of the act of love found in a creature; but when this creature is intelligent and free such an act cannot be elicited without its consent.

Among creatures, the summit of this love that goes back to

God is the Immaculata, the one being totally without any stain of sin, all beautiful, all divine. At no time did her will ever deviate from God's will. With all its strength, her will was always at one with his. In her there came about the marvelous union of God with creation. The Father gave her his Son, as to his spouse, the Son came down into her virginal womb to become her Child; in her the Holy Spirit miraculously fashioned the body of Jesus and made her soul his own dwelling place, penetrating her whole being in such an ineffable manner that the expression "Spouse of the Holy Spirit" is far from adequate to express the life of the Spirit in her and through her. In Jesus there are two natures, divine and human, but one single Person who is God; here on the contrary we have two natures and two persons, the Holy Spirit and the Immaculata, but united in a union that defies all human expression.

The Holy Spirit does not confer any grace, the Father does not give supernatural life to any soul by the Son and the Holy Spirit, unless these gifts are bestowed through the Mediatrix of all grace, the Immaculata, who cooperates in the giving, and distributes them as she wills. She obtains from God all the treasures of grace, as belonging to her, and she distributes them to whomsoever she wills, as she wills.

The fruit of the love of God and of the Immaculata is Jesus, the Son of God and of man, the Mediator between God and man. Just as the Son from all eternity is, so to speak, the mediator between the Father and the Holy Spirit, so too Jesus, the incarnate Son, becomes the direct Mediator between the Father and the Holy Spirit (who is so to speak, as though he were incarnate), and the Immaculata, the Representative and spiritual Mother of all humanity. And it is by her and not otherwise that the love of creatures can rise to Jesus, and by him go back to the Father. We don't always realize this, yet such is the case.

Very naturally, in ordinary life, souls will turn to the Immaculata, to the Holy Spirit, to Jesus, to the eternal Word and to our Heavenly Father; but the more they come to understand that all their acts of love are addressed to the Father as to their ultimate end; that by union with the Immaculata these acts acquire perfect purity; that Jesus will enrich them with an infinite value that makes them capable of procuring the greatest glory to God the Father, then the more these souls will burn with love for Jesus and Mary.

The soul gives all its acts of love to the Immaculata, not as though she were a simple intermediary, but as though she acquired them as her own, completely; for the soul understands that the Immaculata will then offer these acts to Jesus as though they were hers, and hence spotless, immaculate and so he can offer them to the Father.

In this way the soul will belong more and more perfectly to the Immaculata, just as the Immaculata herself belongs to Jesus, and Jesus to his Father.

And even as the flux and reflux of love constitute the very life of God in the bosom of the Trinity, so too will it be between the Creator and the creature which turns back to the Creator from whom it sprang forth.

Mediatrix of All Graces

The Immaculata has left this earth, but her life has only grown the richer; and it develops and flourishes more and more in the lives of Christians. If all the souls that have lived on this earth, and all those that still struggle here could make known the all-powerful influence the Immaculata has exercised on them, and her maternal solicitude for these souls redeemed by the precious Blood of her divine Son, what an incalculable number of volumes would be required! All these people would recount only what they had been able to discover as special graces received through Mary. But in fact every grace that comes to a soul comes from her hands for she is the Mediatrix of all graces; and at every moment new graces penetrate into the souls of men. There are graces which enlighten the intellect, which strengthen the will, which draw us towards what is good. There are ordinary and extraordinary graces; some directly concern our natural life while others have to do with the sanctification of our souls. Only at the Last Judgment, only in Heaven will we discover with what loving attention our heavenly mother watched over each one of us without ceasing, over every soul individually, because all are her children. She strives to shape them after the model of Jesus, her First-born, the archetype of all sanctity, the Man-God.

The Development of the Dogma

It is a fact that from the first instant of her existence the Mother of God never experienced the stain of Original Sin, and that from the earliest days of the Church the faithful acknowledged that our most Holy Mother was the purest of creatures, purer than the angels, entirely free from the least stain of sin.

Now God, who desired to glorify his Immaculate Mother more and more allowed it to happen during the Middle Ages that theologians should scrutinize more closely the texts of Holy Scripture, without succeeding in grasping the link between this truth of Mary's exemption from Original Sin and the inspired words: "In Adam all men have sinned." So they labored long to discover the truth about this matter.

Many attempts were made; many discussions took place. Among others, the Franciscan school especially defended and spread the thesis that in truth the most Blessed Virgin, from the first instant of her conception, had never known the slightest taint of Original Sin, and that her soul had never been subject to Satan's empire. Such was the Franciscan position.

. . . The Council of Trent made it clear in its canons that Original Sin affected all our race, with the exception of the Virgin Mary.

Then, after so many centuries, the time came when Holy Church reached the conviction that this truth could be definitely affirmed for the greater glory of the most Blessed Virgin and the greater good of the faithful. Pius IX, by his Bull *Ineffabilis Deus*, defined this truth as a dogma of faith.

> For the honor of the Holy and Undivided Trinity, for the glory and honor of the Virgin Mother of God, for the exaltation of the Catholic faith . . . by the authority of our Lord Jesus Christ, we declare, pronounce and define that the doctrine which holds that the Blessed Virgin Mary, from the first instant of her conception, and by a singular grace and privilege of God, in view of the merits of Jesus Christ, the Savior of the human race, was preserved from every stain of Original Sin, is a doctrine revealed by God; and that consequently it must be firmly and constantly believed by all the faithful.

About the same time there was an answering echo to all this in the world: the revelation of the Miraculous Medal, the conversion of Alphonse Ratisbonne, and the apparitions of the Immaculata at Lourdes.

The "Immaculate Conception," Her True Name

To Bernadette's repeated request, the Immaculata replied by revealing her true name when she said, "I am the Immaculate Conception." To no one else does such a name properly belong.

When God revealed his name to Moses, he said: "I am the One who is" (Ex 3:14). For God exists from all eternity and to all eternity. His being is unlimited, transcending all time, under whatsoever aspect. Whatever exists apart from God is not "being" itself, but receives its being from him. Thus the Immaculata also began to exist in time.

Among the creatures which began to exist, the angels and our first parents came into being without having been conceived. Mary, on the contrary, like all ordinary humans, began to exist when she was conceived. Jesus Christ, the Man-God, also began his human life by an act of conception. But we should rather say of him that he was conceived, not that he is a "conception," because as the Son of God he exists without a beginning, whereas Mary, since she began in a conception, is different from him, and like all other human beings. But from the first instant of her existence she was distinguished from all the rest of humankind by the fact that their conceptions are sullied by Original Sin, since they are conceived by descendants of our first parents who sinned; Mary's conception, on the contrary, is entirely exempt from this general law; her conception was immaculate.

She does therefore have a full right to the name "Immaculate Conception;" this is indeed her true name.

She is God's Instrument

Of herself, Mary is nothing, even as all other creatures are; but by God's gift she is the most perfect of creatures, the most perfect image of God's divine being in a purely human creature.

She comes, then, from the Father, through the Son and the Holy Spirit, as from her Creator who, out of nothing, calls into being creatures made in his own image, the image of the Holy Trinity. These creatures are limited; yet God likes to find in them the image of himself which they bear. These beings, endowed with reason and free will, know and acknowledge that they come from God and receive everything from him: what they are, what they can do, what they possess moment by moment. In return, they show him their love, both on account of what they receive from him, and because he, God, the infinite perfection, is worthy of infinite love. . . .

The Immaculata never knew the slightest stain; in other words, her love was always full, without flaw. She loved God with all her being, and from the first instant of her existence her love united her with God so perfectly that on the day of the Annunciation the Angel could say to her, "Full of grace! the Lord is with thee!" (cf. Lk 1:28). She is, then, God's creature, God's image, God's child, and in all these respects she is all this in the most perfect manner possible among the ranks of mere creatures.

She is God's instrument. With full consciousness and total willingness she allows God to govern her; she consents to his will, desires only what he desires, and acts according to his will in the most perfect manner, without failing, without ever turning aside from his will. She makes perfect use of the powers and privileges God has given her, so as to fulfill always and in everything whatever God wants of her, purely for love of God, One and Three. This love of God reaches such a peak that it bears the divine fruits proper to God's own love. Her love for God brings her to such a level of union with him that she becomes the Mother of God. The Father confides to her his Son; the Son descends into her womb; and the Holy Spirit fashions out of her perfectly pure body the very Body of Jesus.

Appendix 3

ERECTION OF THE MI AS AN INTERNATIONAL PUBLIC ASSOCIATION

October 16, 1997
Decree of the Pontifical Council for the Laity

I N CONFORMITY WITH THE REQUEST OF THE PIOUS UNION of the Militia of the Immaculate for erection as an international public Association, submitted to the Pontifical Council for the Laity by letter dated 29 August 1996 (Prot. N. 79/96) from the Procurator General of the Order of Friars Minor Conventual, on the petition of the Minister General of the same Order;

Bearing in mind the long and meritorious history associated with the Militia of the Immaculate, founded on 16 October 1917, and whose founder, Fr. Maximilian M. Kolbe, OFM CONV., was later declared a saint and martyr by His Holiness John Paul II (10 October 1982). Erected as a Pious Union on 2 January 1922 by the Vicariate of Rome, the Militia of the Immaculate has received the particular attention and special interest of the Supreme Pontiffs. Among the examples of this attention and interest are the Brief of Pius XI (18 December 1926), which grants indulgences and privileges, and the subsequent Brief of the same Pontiff *Die XVIII mensis Decembris* (23 April 1927), by which the Militia of the Immaculate is raised to a Primary Pious Union. On 8 November 1975, the Pontifical Council for the Laity approved its General Statues and this approbation was renewed on 20 December 1980 *ad experimentum usque ad accommodationem novo Codici juris canonici*;

Having noted with appreciation the subsequent updating of the Statues to bring them in line with the new canonical legislation;

Considering that the Militia of the Immaculate is present today on five continents and in 46 nations, with many canonically erected offices, 27 National Centers and various works of Christian formation and spreading the Gospel, already reaching a total membership that nears four million;

Welcoming with gratitude the definition given by the same Fr. Kolbe to the Militia of the Immaculate: "*A global vision of Catholic life under a new form, consisting in the bond with the Immaculate, our universal Mediatrix before Jesus*" (Kolbe's Writings 1220);

Valuing greatly the scope of the Militia of the Immaculate, "*universal like its mission*", according to what is proposed in the new statutory texts:

1. ...collaborate in the conversion of all, so that "through the intercession of the Virgin Mary, Queen of the Apostles, all peoples might be led as soon as possible to awareness of the truth" (AG 42), to observance of the law of God and union with the Church, "so that with the help of the Mother of God they may be one" (OE 30; MC 33);

2. ...collaborate in the sanctification of all persons and each person in particular, after the example of the Immaculate, in Whom the Church "joyfully contemplates, as in a faultless image, what she as a whole, wishes and hopes to be" (SC 103); and in that way

3. ...obtain the greatest glory for the Most Holy and Undivided Trinity (cf LG 69);

Noting that the Militia of the Immaculate is still under the "*altius moderamen*" of the Minister General of the Franciscan Order of the Friars Minor Conventual and that it has among its most avid supporters and enthusiastic members not a few Most Eminent Cardinals, Most Excellent Bishops and other prelates;

Having closely examined the new General Statutes elaborated by the International Administration of the Militia of the Immaculate;

after ample consultation:

The Pontifical Council for the Laity decrees the erection of the Militia of the Immaculate as an *International Public Association*, in accordance with can. 312, 1, 1 et seq. of the Code of Canon Law, approving at the same time its General Statutes in conformity with the original text presented and filed in the Archives of the Dicastery.

Stanislaw Rylko, Secretary
J. Francis Stafford, President

Vatican City, October 16, 1997
80th Anniversary of the Foundation of the MI

Consecrate Yourself to Mary

Why Should I Consecrate Myself? Consecrating yourself to Mary will be one of the most important days of your life. You will be placing yourself under the mantle of her protective care as the Immaculate Conception, Mother of the Church and Mediatrix of All Graces. Through consecration Our Lady will enlighten your mind, guide your will, empower your efforts and intercede for you in a special way before the Father.

Why Should I Join the MI? By joining St. Maximilian Kolbe's Militia of the Immaculata (MI), you will have the support that comes from being a member of an international movement of spiritual renewal. You will have access to MI conferences and resources, to its national magazine, *Immaculata*, and to regular mailings from the national office on how to better live out your consecration.

How Do I Join the MI? Select a day on which to consecrate yourself to Mary, preferably a Marian feast day. On that day, recite the **MI Prayer of Consecration (page 186)**, before an image of Our Lady if possible. Fill out and mail in an enrollment form to the MI national center.

Prepare for your consecration by spiritual reading, praying the Rosary, Confession, and, if possible, attending Mass and receiving Communion on the day of enrollment. After making your consecration, ask Mary and St. Maximilian to show you how to best serve the Lord from this moment on.

YES! Enroll me in the MI.

☐ I have fulfilled the conditions for membership and will pursue the purposes of the MI. Please enroll me on this date:

_____

☐ I wish to support the work of the MI movement with a gift of $ _____

Mr./Mrs./Ms./other_____

Address_____

City_____ State _____ Zip _____

Phone (_____) _____ Date of birth ____/____/____

- -

☐ I have fulfilled the conditions for membership and will pursue the purposes of the MI. Please enroll me on this date:

_____

☐ I wish to support the work of the MI movement with a gift of $ _____

Mr./Mrs./Ms./other_____

Address_____

City_____ State _____ Zip _____

Phone (_____) _____ Date of birth ____/____/____

Make your gift payable to the Militia of the Immaculata.
Cut out or photocopy this form, mail it to the MI National Center—
Marytown, 1600 W. Park Ave., Libertyville, IL 60048

Prayer of Marian Consecration
of St. Maximilian Kolbe

O Immaculata, Queen of Heaven and earth, refuge of sinners and our most loving Mother, God has willed to entrust the entire order of mercy to you. I, [name], a repentant sinner, cast myself at your feet humbly imploring you to take me with all that I am and have, wholly to yourself as your possession and property. Please make of me, of all my powers of soul and body, of my whole life, death and eternity, whatever most pleases you.

If it pleases you, use all that I am and have without reserve, wholly to accomplish what was said of you: "She will crush your head," and, "You alone have destroyed all heresies in the world." Let me be a fit instrument in your immaculate and merciful hands for introducing and increasing your glory to the maximum in all the many strayed and indifferent souls, and thus help extend as far as possible the blessed kingdom of the most Sacred Heart of Jesus. For wherever you enter you obtain the grace of conversion and growth in holiness, since it is through your hands that all graces come to us from the most Sacred Heart of Jesus.

V. Allow me to praise you, O sacred Virgin.
R. Give me strength against your enemies.